LEARNING
About God

Essential Christian Concepts
for Preschoolers

LEARNING
About God

Essential Christian Concepts
for Preschoolers

---

52 Versatile Lesson Plans

wesleyan
publishing
house

Indianapolis, Indiana

Copyright © 2005 by Wesleyan Publishing House
Published by Wesleyan Publishing House
Indianapolis, Indiana 46250
Printed in the United States of America

ISBN-13: 978-0-89827-289-5
ISBN-10: 0-89827-289-0

Written by Mary Miller and Colleen Derr.

Library of Congress Cataloging-in-Publication Data

Learning about God : essential Christian concepts for preschoolers : 52
versatile lesson plans.
    p. cm.
 Includes bibliographical references.
 ISBN-13: 978-0-89827-289-5 (pbk.)
 1. Christian education of preschool children. I. Wesleyan Publishing
House.
 BV1475.8.L38 2005
 268'.432—dc22
                  2005011169

Contents

How to Use This Book

The spiritual formation of children is a critical task that includes the development of their spirit, mind, relationships, and behavior—heart, head, hands, and habits. This book contains fifty-two versatile session plans to assist you in developing a child's *mind* by teaching basic truths of the Christian faith. To be successful in forming a child spiritually, instruction must be reinforced by modeled behavior and encouragement outside the teaching setting. These lessons are intended to be one part of a holistic approach to the discipleship of children. They are designed for use primarily as a supplement to existing discipleship curricula.

Here's how to make the most of this resource.

Step 1: Choose a Setting

Examine your church's overall children's ministry program and select the setting where this material will be most effective. Some possibilities for use are—

- Alongside existing Sunday school curriculum
- During the children's sermon portion of a worship service
- As one feature in a children's church program
- As the teaching material for a midweek children's program
- As the entire program of a specialized class devoted to discipleship

Step 2: Choose a Teaching Plan

Based on the setting that you have selected, determine how much time will be available for instruction. These session plans are versatile and offer teaching options ranging from five minutes to one hour. Based on the available time for instruction, choose one of four teaching options.

Option 1: 5-Minute Sessions

Include these session elements:

- Say (3–5 minutes)
- Action Point (1–2 minutes)

Possible uses:

- Add-on element to Sunday school curriculum
- Children's sermon for a worship service

Option 2: 15-Minute Sessions

Include these session elements:

- Memory Verse (5 minutes)
- Say (5 minutes)
- Action Point (3 minutes)
- Prayer (2 minutes)

Possible uses:

- Add-on to existing Sunday school curriculum
- Teaching portion of a midweek children's program
- One element of a children's church program

Option 3: 30-Minute Sessions

Include these session elements:

- Memory Verse (5 minutes)
- Say (5 minutes)
- Action Point (3 minutes)
- One Activity Option (7–10 minutes)
- Prayer (5 minutes)
- Bridge (2 minutes)

Possible uses:

- Teaching portion of a midweek children's program
- Teaching portion of a children's church program
- Small group study
- Home school lesson

Option 4: 60-Minute Sessions

Sixty-minute sessions call for the use of all session elements as well as additional resources, many of which are included in this book. In addition, some session elements are suggested here which do not appear in each printed session plan.

Use this suggested structure for a 60-minute session.

- Sharing Time—Build relationships by sharing life experiences that relate to the session content. (5–10 minutes)
- Worship Songs—See Music Resources section (page 121) for suggestions (10 minutes)
- Memory Verse (5–10 minutes)
- Say (5 minutes)
- Action Point (3 minutes)

- Activities (15–25 minutes)
- Prayer—See How To Teach Children to Pray section (page 125) for varied approaches (10 minutes)
- Bridge (2 minutes)

Possible uses:

- Midweek children's program
- Children's church program
- Small group study
- Catechism class

Step 3: Conduct an Assessment

Use the Assessment Tool to determine the knowledge base of your children. The tool will reveal which concepts the students already grasp and which need to be reinforced.

Step 4: Create a Teaching Calendar

Use the Teaching Calendar (page 144) to plan your activities for the quarter or year, including the concepts to be taught, session elements to include, activity options selected, and teaching tools to be used.

Step 5: Prepare to Teach

Become familiar with the elements of these sessions and spend adequate time preparing to communicate the biblical concept. There is room for lesson notes in the gray sidebar of each page.

- *Concept*—the Biblical truth to be communicated.
- *Memory Verse*—a variety of memorization activities are included in this book.
- *Before You Begin*—pre-session preparation suggestions.
- *Teaching Points*—primary points to emphasize during the session
- *Say*—a five-minute presentation of the biblical concept, intended to be either read aloud or summarized during the session
- *Activities Options*—student activities that may be used during the session to reinforce the concept experientially.
- *Action Point*—a question, challenge, or suggested action to assist children in applying the concept to life.
- *Prayer*—a suggested prayer to assist the leader in verbalizing our response to God's truth.
- *Bridge*—a statement, intended to be read aloud or summarized, that arouses interest in the next session.

Also become familiar with the additional resources provided in this book and plan ways to use them during the teaching sessions. Additional elements are—

- *Learning Concepts*—a listing of the fifty-two concepts presented in this book, arranged by topic (page 10).

- *Competency Goals for Preschoolers*—skills that children at this age level should be working toward mastering (page 11).

- *Developmental Characteristics of Preschoolers*—insights on how children learn and develop that will enhance your teaching and make it most beneficial to children (page 116).

- *Preschooler Assessment Tool*—a pre-test to clarify the areas in which children need most intensive instruction. This tool may be used informally in one-to-one conversation or in a group setting. It also serves as a post-test to evaluate learning (page 119).

- *Preschool Scripture Memory Ideas*—a variety of ideas to help teach Scripture verses to preschool children (page 121).

- *How to Lead a Child to Christ*—a basic, step-by-step approach to leading a child to Christ (page 123).

- *How to Teach Children to Pray*—a variety of methods for introducing children to prayer (page 125).

- *Music Resources*—a list of age-appropriate worship music options (page 127).

- *Additional Resources*—a list of tools to assist in teaching children and organizing children's ministry (page 128).

- *Reproducible Activity Items*—supplemental items provided for some lessons (page 130).

- *Teaching Calendar*—a tool for developing a teaching plan and tracking progress (page 144).

Step 6: Assess Learning

After completing the teaching cycle, reassess the children's knowledge using the assessment tool. Identify areas that may need to be revisited and reviewed.

Teaching Tips

- Understand the biblical concepts. It is vital to spend time in prayer, Bible study, and preparation for each lesson. Read the recommended scriptures and reach a solid understanding of each truth.

- Understand your students. In order to effectively communicate these concepts and to take advantage of the most appropriate teaching tools, it is vital to understand where children are developmentally. Get to know your students so that you can communicate God's truth to them.

Learning Concepts

God

1. God is real.
2. God is good.
3. God made me.
4. God takes care of me.
5. God made the world.
6. God takes care of the world.
7. God hears us talk to Him.
8. God gives us rules.
9. God can do anything.
10. God knows everything.

Scripture

11. The Bible is a special book.
12. The Bible tells us about God and Jesus.
13. The stories in the Bible are true.
14. The Bible helps me know what to do.

Self

15. God made me special.
16. God loves me.
17. God made my family.
18. God wants me to love Him.
19. God wants me to obey Him.
20. I can know right from wrong.

Jesus

21. Jesus is God's son.
22. Jesus was born as a baby.
23. Jesus grew up, just like me.
24. Jesus always obeyed God.
25. Jesus taught people about God.

26. Jesus loves me.
27. Jesus died on the cross.
28. Jesus is alive.

Salvation

29. Sin is doing wrong.
30. Everyone has disobeyed God.
31. God wants to forgive me.
32. Jesus died for my sin.
33. Jesus is my forever friend.
34. I am part of God's family.
35. We can live with Jesus in heaven.

Church

36. People at church love God.
37. We worship God at church.
38. We learn about Jesus at church.
39. We worship God by singing and praying.
40. We worship God by learning His Word.
41. We help others at church.

The Christian Life

42. I can pray for others.
43. I can bring an offering to church.
44. I can invite a friend to church.
45. God helps me do what is right.
46. I can help others.
47. I can grow like Jesus.
48. I can love my family.
49. I can ask God for help.
50. I can tell my friends about Jesus.
51. I am joyful because I know Jesus.
52. I will go to heaven with Jesus.

Competency Goals for Preschoolers

Preschoolers Can . . .

1. Treat the Bible with respect.

2. Accept Jesus as their Savior when ready.

3. Help others.

4. Respect and obey parents.

5. Pray.

6. Help take care of God's world.

7. Bring offerings.

8. Invite a friend to church.

God

Memory Verse
Be still, and know
that I am God.
Psalm 46:10

1 God is real.

Before You Begin

- Read 1 Kings 19:11–13, Psalm 102: 25–27, Romans 1:20, and Revelation 1:8.
- Review the Teaching Points to familiarize yourself with the ideas to emphasize in this session.
- Read the session plan and select the elements that you will include.
- Choose a Bible memorization technique from those listed in Section 1. Be sure to vary your teaching technique from session to session.
- If you choose to include a learning activity, gather the materials you will need.
  - For Activity 1 you will need a ball (or another object that the children can hold and touch) and paper folded into a fan shape or an electric fan.
  - For Activity 2 you will need pictures of nature and animals.

Teaching Points

- We can know God is real.
- We can see what God made.
- We can hear God speak.

Say

How do you know that something is real? If you can see it, do you know it is real? If you can touch it, do you know it is real? Can you know that something is real even if you can't see it or touch it? We cannot see God or touch Him like I can see and touch you, but we can know that God is very real.

The Bible says, "God created the heavens and the earth" (Gen. 1:1). God made the sun in the sky, the trees, and the flowers; He even made you and me! We know God is real because we can see the world that He made.

We know God is real because we can hear when He talks to us. God talks to us most of all through the Bible. It's His written Word. God also talks to us through the words of people who have known God longer than we have. And sometimes God speaks to us through our conscience, that "little voice" or feeling, which tells us if something is good or bad. Our memory verse tells us that God wants us to be still and know that He is God (Ps. 46:10). Sometimes it is very hard to be still! But we are not able to hear God if we are not listening to the Bible, other Christians, and His "whisper."

When we see all the wonderful things God made, we can know that God is real.

Activity Options

Activity 1: *Is it real?* Show the children a ball or other small object. How do we know the ball is real? We can see it and touch it. Use a paper fan to demonstrate that some things are real but cannot be seen. Show the children how to wave the fan gently in front of them (a small electric fan also works well for this activity). The air is real; we feel it but we can't see it. We don't see God with our eyes, but we know that He is real when we see what He does and hear what He says.

Activity 2: *Take a walk!* Take a walk to look at the beauty of God's creation. Encourage the children to talk about what they see and like. Talk about how seeing the beautiful world helps us to know there is a God. If your class cannot take a walk outside, find pictures of natural scenes, plants, and animals in books or magazines. Let the children look and comment on the pictures.

Action Point

God wants you to know He is real. Can you be still and listen to God this week?

Prayer

Dear God, thank You that You want us to know You are real and that we can see Your work in the world You made. Help us to be still and listen so that You can speak to us. Amen.

For Next Time

We have learned that God is real, but have you ever wondered what God is like? We'll learn more next time.

God

Memory Verse
Taste and see that
the Lord is good.
Psalm 34:8

2 God is good.

Before You Begin

- Read Exodus 33:19–23; 34:6–7, Psalm 145, and Romans 8:28.
- Review the Teaching Points to familiarize yourself with the ideas to emphasize in this session.
- Read the session plan and select the elements that you will include.
- Choose a Bible memorization technique from those listed in Section 1. Be sure to vary your teaching technique from session to session.
- If you choose to include a learning activity, gather the materials you will need.
  - For Activity 1 you will need cookies or some other small treat.

Teaching Points

- God is good.
- God invites us to see that He is good.
- God is good in every way.
- God is good to everyone.

Say

Have you ever wanted to try some food you've never eaten before? Did you look at it and wonder if it tasted good? Sometimes, as we learn about God, we might wonder what He is really like. God invites us to try Him out, to "taste and see that the Lord is good" (Ps. 34:8). We can't taste God the way we taste food, but we can trust Him to help us each day. As we try trusting Him, we will see that He is good.

God is good all the time and in every way. We can sometimes make mistakes, but God never does. We can sometimes choose to do wrong, but God never does any wrong. God never even has a bad thought. God doesn't just do good things, He is good.

Because God is good by nature, He is also good to everyone. The Bible

14

says, "The Lord is good to all; he has compassion on all he has made" (Ps. 145:9). God cares about us and what will happen to us. That doesn't mean that nothing bad will happen to us. But because He loves us so much, God can even use bad things to help us trust and love Him more. The Bible says, "We know that in all things God works for the good of those who love him" (Rom. 8:28). If we will trust Him to do us good and try to do what He says, we will see that God is very good.

Activity Options

Activity 1: *Taste and see*. Invite the children to taste some cookies, fruit, or other treat to see if it is good. Talk about how we can "taste" or try out God to learn that He is good. Some ways include trusting Him, even when things go wrong, obeying Him when we know what He wants us to do, and learning how to live to please Him.

Activity 2: *God is good.* Teach the children the following phrases. You say, "God is good." The children respond with, "All the time." Then, when you say, "And all the time," the children respond, "God is good." You can do these phrases at various times unannounced until the children learn to respond automatically.

Action Point

Why not try God out this week by putting your trust in Him? You'll see that He is good.

Prayer

Dear God, we thank You that You are good. Thank You for inviting us to try You out. Help us to trust You, knowing that You will do us good. Amen.

For Next Time

Everything God does is good, including how He made each one of us. We will learn about that next time.

God

Memory Verse
I praise you because
I am fearfully and
wonderfully made.
Psalm 139:14

3 God made me.

Before You Begin

■ Read Genesis 1:26–31; Psalm 139, and Ephesians 2:10.
■ Review the Teaching Points to familiarize yourself with the ideas to emphasize in this session.
■ Read the session plan and select the elements that you will include.
■ Choose a Bible memorization technique from those listed in Section 1. Be sure to vary your teaching technique from session to session.
■ If you choose to include a learning activity, gather the materials you will need.
  • For Activity 1 you will need one or more handheld mirrors, paper, and pencils.
  • For Activity 2 you will need drawing paper, a marker, and crayons.

Teaching Points

■ God made me one-of-a-kind.
■ God made me just the way I am.
■ God made me to be like Him.

Say

When we look in a mirror, what do we see? We see ourselves. We also see a one-of-a-kind creation made by God himself. God made each of us. He planned how He wanted us to be, and He put us together. Even before we were born, God knew what we would look like, what things we would like and dislike, even what things we would be able to do well. In the Bible, King David described how God made him by saying, "You created my inmost being; you knit me together" (Ps. 139:13).

The Bible says, "We are God's workmanship" (Eph. 2:10). Imagine how boring it would be if everyone looked the same, liked the same things, and talked the same way. But God is a very good artist, and He made each of us different. He gave some of us dark skin and some of us light skin. He gave some of us blue eyes and some of us brown eyes. We all like different things and have different abilities too.

We've already learned that God is good. Because God is good, we can be sure that He made us in the very best way. God made us "in his own image" (Gen. 1:27). That means He made us to be like Him. That is a very good reason to praise Him. We really are wonderfully made!

Activity Options

Activity 1: *We're all different.* Have one or more handheld mirrors so the children can look at themselves. Talk about how God made each of us different. Count and keep track on paper how many students have blue eyes, how many have dark hair, who has freckles, and who doesn't. You can come up with as many categories as you like, but be sure everyone fits into at least one category.

Activity 2: *God made me portrait.* Ahead of time, use a marker to write the memory verse on the bottom of a piece of drawing paper. Make one for each student in your class. Give each child a piece of drawing paper and some crayons and let them draw a self-portrait. Hang the portraits in the classroom, or encourage the children to hang them up at home.

Action Point

God made each of us in a wonderful way. Will you remember to thank and praise Him every day for the way He made you?

Prayer

Dear God, thank You so much for making us just the way You did. We praise You that You made each of us different but that we are all made to be like You. Amen.

For Next Time

God made us, but does He care what happens to us? Can we trust God to take care of us? We'll find out next time.

God

Memory Verse
He cares for those
who trust in him.
Nahum 1:7

4 God takes care of me.

Before You Begin

- Read Psalm 103, Jeremiah 29:11, Matthew 6:25–34, and Luke 12:6–7.
- Review the Teaching Points to familiarize yourself with the ideas to emphasize in this session.
- Read the session plan and select the elements that you will include.
- Choose a Bible memorization technique from those listed in Section 1. Be sure to vary your teaching technique from session to session.
- If you choose to include a learning activity, gather the materials you will need.
  - For Activity 1 you will need pictures from magazines of things we need, scissors, one large sheet of paper, glue, and markers.

Teaching Points

- God takes care of me.
- I am important to God.
- God knows what I need.
- God cares what happens to me.

Say

Can you guess how many hairs you have on your head? God knows the answer. Do you know how many birds live in your yard? God knows where every bird is in the whole world, yet we are more important than the birds to Him. We are important to God, and He takes care of us.

Let's think of some things we all need. We need food and water; we need rest when we're tired. We need family and friends, and we need to feel loved. We have many needs but God knows all about them. The Bible says, "He knows how we are formed" (Ps. 103:14). If God knows how we are formed, He knows how to give us what we need. We don't have to worry if God will take care of us. Jesus tells us, "Do not worry, saying, 'What shall we eat?' or 'What shall we drink' or 'What shall we wear?'" (Matt. 6:31).

Jesus said that we don't have to worry about these things because, "your heavenly Father knows that you need them" (Matt. 6:32).

God has plans for your life as you grow up. He plans how to care for you. The Bible tells us, "'I know the plans I have for you', declares the Lord, 'plans to prosper you and not to harm you, plans to give you hope and a future'" (Jer. 29:11). We can trust God to take care of us all the days of our lives. God takes care of you.

Activity Options

Activity 1: *God cares for me collage.* Ahead of time, cut pictures of things we need from magazines. Some examples are food, a place to live, and clothing. Include pictures of family, someone laughing, singing, etc. Help the children glue the pictures to one large sheet of paper. Talk about how God gives us the things we need. Write the memory verse on the bottom of the collage and hang it in your classroom.

Activity 2: *God cares for me chant.* Have everyone sit in a circle. Start the chant by saying, "God cares for me. He gives me ____." Fill in the blank with some way God cares for you. Have the children clap as you say each word. Then say, "How does God care for you?" As you say this, point to someone else in the circle. Help that child repeat the chant, changing the word in the blank. Continue, giving each child at least one turn to say the chant and point to someone else.

Action Point

You are important to God, and He knows how to give you everything you need. Will you trust Him to take care of you?

Prayer

Dear God, thank You for taking care of us. Help us to trust You for all our needs. Thank You for making plans to take care of us for all our lives. Amen.

For Next Time

God made each of us and knows how to take care of us. Did God make the world we live in? We'll find out next time.

God

Memory Verse
In the beginning God
created the heavens
and the earth.
Genesis 1:1

5 God made the world.

Before You Begin

- Read Genesis 1, Psalm 24:1–2, Jeremiah 10:11–13, and Revelation 4:11.
- Review the Teaching Points to familiarize yourself with the ideas to emphasize in this session.
- Read the session plan and select the elements that you will include.
- Choose a Bible memorization technique from those listed in Section 1. Be sure to vary your teaching technique from session to session.
- If you choose to include a learning activity, gather the materials you will need.
  - For Activity 1 you will need air-dry clay, enough for each child to have a small amount.
  - For Activity 2 you will need pieces of drawing paper with the memory verse written on them, leaves, and crayons.

Teaching Points

- God made the world.
- The world belongs to God.
- We should thank God for making the world.

Say

The very first thing the Bible tells us about God is that He made the world. There is no one stronger or wiser than God. The Bible says, "God made the earth by his power; he founded the world by his wisdom" (Jer. 10:12). He didn't make the world out of things that were already there. God made the world out of nothing. God spoke, and the world and everything in it was made.

Have you ever taken a plain piece of paper and drawn a beautiful picture? How did you feel about your picture? Were you proud? Your work of art is something you can call your own. God made the world, so the world belongs to Him. The Bible says, "The earth is the Lord's, and everything in it, the world, and all who live in it" (Ps. 24:1). That means every plant, every animal, the mountains, the stars, and even you and I belong to God!

God made the world. He made the world to be a beautiful place, and He deserves our praise for it. The Bible says, "You are worthy, our Lord and God, to receive glory and honor and power, for you created all things" (Rev. 4:11). God made the world, and it belongs to Him. Let's remember to praise Him for it.

Activity Options

Activity 1: *What can you make?* Give each child a small lump of air-dry clay. Invite the children to "create" something by shaping the clay into the form of an animal or plant, etc. Talk about how they can shape something out of clay to copy something God made, but only God can make something out of nothing. Talk about how each piece belongs to the child who made it, and the world belongs to God. Allow the pieces to dry completely before sending them home with the children.

Activity 2: *Leaf rubbings.* Ahead of time, write the memory verse on blank paper. Have the children go with you to collect a few leaves or bring a few leaves to class with you. Show the children how to place their paper over the leaves and rub it with the side of a crayon to make a pretty leaf pattern on the paper. Let the children do as many rubbings as time allows.

Action Point

God made the world, and it belongs to Him. What things about the world can you thank God for?

Prayer

Dear God, we are glad You made the world. We know it belongs to You. Help us to remember to thank You for it. Amen.

For Next Time

The world belongs to God, and He can do anything He wants to with it. Next time, we'll learn how God takes care of His world.

God

Memory Verse
In his hand is the life
of every creature.
Job 12:10

6 God takes care of the world.

Before You Begin

- Read Job 38, Matthew 6:26–29 and 8:23–27.
- Review the Teaching Points to familiarize yourself with the ideas to emphasize in this session.
- Read the session plan and select the elements that you will include.
- Choose a Bible memorization technique from those listed in Section 1. Be sure to vary your teaching technique from session to session.
- If you choose to include a learning activity, gather the materials you will need.
  - For Activity 1 you will need a potted plant.

Teaching Points

- God takes care of the world.
- God is in control of the world.
- God watches over the world.

Say

The world is a big place and sometimes scary, but God is in control of the world. Sometimes there are bad storms. Sometimes we wonder what will happen. God takes care of the world. Noah lived through a big flood. Noah trusted God, and God kept him and his family safe. God promised Noah, "As long as the earth endures, seedtime and harvest, cold and heat, summer and winter, day and night will never cease" (Gen. 8:22). God can make a promise like that because He is in control of the world.

God takes care of the world. He causes the sun to shine and gives the wild animals their food. He sends rain to water the flowers and makes them grow. Rabbits have a warm place to live, and birds have lots of worms to eat.

God watches over the world and knows what happens to every creature. A sparrow is a very small bird, but the Bible says that, "not one of them is forgotten by God (Luke 12:6). Our memory verse tells us that the lives of every living creature are in His hands. God watches and sees what happens to every creature. God takes care of the world.

Activity Options

Activity 1: *A plant to care for.* Bring a small potted plant to the classroom. The children can look at it and touch it carefully. Talk about how a plant needs water, sunlight, and plant food. Explain to the children that just as God cares for the world, they can care for the plant. Let the children find a place in the classroom for the plant. Over the following weeks, have the children take turns watering the plant, giving it plant food, or turning it in the sunshine.

Activity 2: *Caring for the world.* Ask the children to help you think of ways to help take care of God's world. Some good examples include throwing the trash into a trash can instead of on the ground, being kind to animals, recycling, and leaving wild plants and animals alone. Explore inside and outside your church or building to find out where the trash cans and recycling bins (if applicable) are. Let the children help throw away any scraps of paper littering the area.

Action Point

God takes care of the world. The next time you are worried about a big storm, can you remember that God is in control?

Prayer

Dear God, thank You for taking care of the world. Help us to remember that we are safe in Your hands no matter what happens because You are in control. Amen.

For Next Time

God takes care of the whole world, but He's not too busy to listen to us. We'll talk about that next time.

God

7 God hears us talk to him.

Before You Begin

■ Read 1 Kings 8:22–53, Psalm 116:1–2, Jeremiah 33:3, and Matthew 6:5–15.
■ Review the Teaching Points to familiarize yourself with the ideas to emphasize in this session.
■ Read the session plan and select the elements that you will include.
■ Choose a Bible memorization technique from those listed in Section 1. Be sure to vary your teaching technique from session to session.
■ If you choose to include a learning activity, gather the materials you will need.
  ● For Activity 1 you will need crayons and the reproducible prayer reminder pattern found on page 131.

Teaching Points

■ God hears us talk to Him.
■ God wants us to talk to Him.
■ God hears us anytime.
■ God will answer us.

Say

Would you like to talk to God? Talking to God is called prayer, and God wants us to talk, or pray, to Him. God wants us to tell Him what we need. In the Bible, Jesus says, "Ask and it will be given to you" (Matt. 7:7). It doesn't matter if we're not sure what to ask for because Jesus also said, "Your Father knows what you need before you ask him" (Matt. 6:8).

God will hear us anytime we pray. We do not have to be in church to talk to God. We do not have to wait for Sunday to talk to Him. We don't even have to pray out loud. King David wrote in the Bible, "The Lord will hear when I call to Him" (Ps. 4:3). We can be sure of the same thing; God will hear us no matter where we are or when we pray.

God not only hears us; He also answers us. God says in the Bible, "'Call to me and I will answer you'" (Jer. 33:3). This doesn't mean God will give us anything we ask for. God loves us and knows better than we do how to answer our prayers. Sometimes His answer is "no." Sometimes His answer is "wait." We can trust God's answers because He is good. Let's remember to pray because God will always hear us when we talk to Him.

Activity Options

Activity 1: *Prayer reminder.* Give each child a copy of the prayer reminder pattern found in the Reproducible Activities Items section. Point out to the children the boxes beneath the picture, labeled for each day of the week. Talk about how important it is to talk to God every day. Let the children color the picture. Tell them to take the picture home to remind them to talk to God every day. Show them how to mark an "x" in each box as they pray each day.

Activity 2: *Prayer practice.* Help the children begin to learn to pray by having a prayer time with them in class. Help the children with some ideas about what to talk to God about. Start a simple prayer and encourage the children to add their own phrases, such as praises or simple requests. Finish the prayer time by thanking God for always hearing us when we talk to Him.

Action Point

God will hear and answer us when we pray. Will you remember to talk to God every day?

Prayer

Dear God, thank You for hearing us when we talk to You. Help us to remember to pray to You every day and to trust You for the answers you give. Amen.

For Next Time

God hears us when we talk to Him, but He also expects us to listen to Him when He gives us rules. We'll find out more about that next time.

God

Memory Verse
I will always obey your law,
for ever and ever.
Psalm 119:44

 ## God gives us rules.

Before You Begin

- Read Exodus 20:1–21 and Psalm 119.
- Review the Teaching Points to familiarize yourself with the ideas to emphasize in this session.
- Read the session plan and select the elements that you will include.
- Choose a Bible memorization technique from those listed in Section 1. Be sure to vary your teaching technique from session to session.
- If you choose to include a learning activity, gather the materials you will need.
  - For Activity 1 you will need music and a cassette or CD player.
  - For Activity 2 you will need a picture of a tree (if using that option) and something to represent chaff, such as oatmeal or another small grain.

Teaching Points

- God gives us rules
- God's rules are for our good.
- God expects us to obey His rules.

Say

Imagine standing on the edge of a high cliff. What could we do to keep someone from stepping over the edge and falling? We could put up a fence or boundary to keep people away from the edge. God sets up fences or boundaries to keep us safe. God gives us rules for our good. He knows that doing bad things harm us so He gives us rules to teach us how to live right. The Bible says, "Blessed are they who keep his statutes. . . . They do nothing wrong" (Ps. 119:2–3).

God tells us, "You shall not steal" (Exod. 20:15). That means stealing is wrong, and we should never do it. It is one of God's rules. God says, "Children, obey your parents," (Eph. 6:1). It is one of God's rules, and

26

we should always do it. We may not always understand why God gives us some of His rules, but we can trust Him because He is good.

God expects us to obey His rules. The Bible says that someone who obeys God's rules is like "a tree planted by streams of water" (Ps. 1:3). That tree is strong and will grow. The Bible says that those who don't obey God's rules are like "chaff" (Jer. 13:24). Chaff is the part of grain that blows away in the wind. God gives us rules, and He expects us to obey them because they are for our good.

Activity Options

Activity 1: *No rules*. Play musical chairs without any rules. Put chairs in a circle and play music. Tell the children they can walk in any direction or sit in the chairs; it doesn't matter! Give the children too many chairs or don't take any away. There are no winners, only confusion. Use this activity to demonstrate how rules are important, much more in life than in games, and that without God's rules we would not know what to do. Then play the game correctly.

Activity 2: *Tree or chaff?* Look at a large tree (or show a picture of one). The tree is strong and can't easily be knocked over. Discuss how God's rules make us strong. Use some small grain or bits of some material to represent chaff. Let the children blow some of the "chaff" from their hands. Talk about the differences between the strong tree and the chaff that is easy to lose. The Bible compares people who obey or disobey God's rules to these two items.

Action Point

God gives us good rules to help us live right. Will you choose to obey them?

Prayer

Dear God, thank You for Your good rules. Help us to always obey them so we can be strong and grow to please You more each day. Amen.

For Next Time

God gives us good rules to live by, but is there anything God can't do? We'll find out next time.

God

Memory Verse
Our God is in heaven; he does
whatever pleases him.
Psalm 115:3

9 God can do anything.

Before You Begin

- Read Job 36:26 and 42:1–3, Isaiah 55:8, and Luke 18:24–27.
- Review the Teaching Points to familiarize yourself with the ideas to emphasize in this session.
- Read the session plan and select the elements that you will include.
- Choose a Bible memorization technique from those listed in Section 1. Be sure to vary your teaching technique from session to session.
- If you choose to include a learning activity, gather the materials you will need.
  - For Activity 2 you will need one piece of paper for each child with "Anything" written on one side and "Nothing" written on the other.

Teaching Points

- God has no limits.
- God can do anything.
- God answers to no one.

Say

Do you ever pretend that you are a superhero? Or do you ever pretend that you have power to do things you really can't do? God is the only one who has all power, and He can do anything. There is no one as strong as God. There is no one more powerful. There is nothing He doesn't understand. The Bible says, "How great is God—beyond our understanding!" (Job 36:26). God has no limits.

God can do anything He wants. He is so much greater than we are that we can never really know what He is going to do. God says of himself, "'My thoughts are not your thoughts, neither are your ways my ways'" (Isa. 55:8). God does what He wants to do, but He will always do what is right.

God answers to no one. You may sometimes have to ask your mom, dad, or teacher for permission to do something you want to do. Even grown ups have to answer to others for what they do. But God doesn't ask our permission to do anything or explain to us why He does what He does. The Bible says, "No one can hold back his hand or say to him: 'What have you done?'" (Dan. 4:35). His wisdom is enough to decide what to do and His strength is enough to do it. He is God, and He can do anything.

Activity Options

Activity 1: *God can do anything.* Ask the children to stand and follow along, doing the motions with the words: "God is so big" (stretch arms out to the side). "God is so strong" (raise arms and make fists). "God is so wise" (point to head). "Who can do anything?" (raise hands, palms up). "Only God!" (point upward). Repeat the phrases and the motions several times.

Activity 2: *Anything or nothing.* Give each child a piece of paper with "Anything" written on one side and "Nothing" written on the other. Have the children hold up the paper with the correct side showing to answer the questions you will ask them: "What things can God do?" "What limits does God have?" "What does God have to get permission to do?" "God can do . . . ." (You can also guide the children in asking each other questions like these).

Action Point

God can do anything. Can you think of anything in your life that God needs to do for you?

Prayer

Dear God, we're glad You can do anything. Thank You that what You do is good because You are good. Help us to trust You even when we don't know why You do what You do. Amen.

For Next Time

God has no limits; He can do anything. Is there anything God doesn't know? We'll find out next time.

God

Memory Verse
Nothing in all creation
is hidden from God's sight.
Hebrews 4:13

10 God knows everything.

Before You Begin

- Read Job 21:22, Psalm 139, and Isaiah 46:8–10.
- Review the Teaching Points to familiarize yourself with the ideas to emphasize in this session.
- Read the session plan and select the elements that you will include.
- Choose a Bible memorization technique from those listed in Section 1. Be sure to vary your teaching technique from session to session.
- If you choose to include a learning activity, gather the materials you will need.
  - For Activity 1 you will need binoculars, a magnifying glass, eyeglasses, and a mirror.
  - For Activity 2 you will need the picture of children doing good and bad that can be found on page 132.

Teaching Points

- God knows everything.
- God does not need to learn anything.
- Nothing that happens surprises God.
- God knows everything we think and do.

Say

Do you like to learn things? Children go to school so they can learn things. Even grown-ups can go to school to learn things. Can God learn too? In the Bible, a man named Job asked the question, "Can anyone teach knowledge to God?" (Job 21:22). The answer is no! God does not need to learn anything because He already knows everything.

God knows everything that has already happened. God knows everything that is happening now. God knows everything that is going to happen. God says this about himself: "I make known the end from the beginning" (Isa. 46:10). Since God already knows what will happen, nothing that happens surprises Him.

God knows everything we think and do. He sees everything. No one can keep a secret from Him. God knows what you are thinking and doing right now! The Bible says that God knows when we sit and when we rise (Ps. 139:2). God even knows what you are going to say before you say it. The Bible also says that before a word is even formed on our tongues, God knows it completely (Ps. 139:4). Since God knows what we are thinking and doing, it's best that we think and do things that are pleasing to Him. It is good that God knows everything and that nothing surprises Him. We can trust Him to help us today because He knows what will happen tomorrow.

Activity Options

Activity 1: *God sees.* Show the children a variety of items that people use to see things. Some good examples include binoculars, a magnifying glass, eyeglasses, and a mirror. Talk about the function of each item and how people use these items to help them see. Without these items we would not know as much about some of the things they help us see. Talk about how God sees and knows everything. Nothing is hidden from His sight.

Activity 2: *God knows.* Show your class the picture of children doing good and bad deeds. Talk about what is happening in each picture. Remind the children that God sees everything we do and knows everything we think and say. Talk about how the children in the pictures might behave differently if they knew God was watching them. Challenge the children to remember that God is also always watching them and knows what they are doing.

Action Point

Is there anything that you have done that you think no one knows about? God knows all about it.

Prayer

Dear God, we're glad nothing surprises You. Help us to remember that You see everything we do. Help us to trust You because You know what will happen each day of our lives. Amen.

For Next Time

We've been talking about what the Bible says about God. Next time, we'll talk about what the Bible says about itself.

Scripture

11 The Bible is a special book.

Before You Begin

■ Read Exodus 24:3–4, Isaiah 55:10–11, Hebrews 4:12, and James 1:22–25.
■ Review the Teaching Points to familiarize yourself with the ideas to emphasize in this session.
■ Read the session plan and select the elements that you will include.
■ Choose a Bible memorization technique from those listed in Section 1. Be sure to vary your teaching technique from session to session.
■ If you choose to include a learning activity, gather the materials you will need.
  • For Activity 1 you will need a special guest and a much-used Bible.
  • For Activity 2 you will need one or more Bibles.

Teaching Points

■ The Bible is a special book.
■ The Bible is God's Word.
■ The Bible will last forever.
■ God speaks to us through the Bible.

Say

Think of your favorite book. We like books because they have good stories in them. Some books have good pictures in them. There are a lot of good books. The Bible is sometimes called "the Good Book," but it is not like any other book in the world. The Bible is God's Word. That means that the words in the Bible tell us about God and what God wants us to know.

Because God is eternal and the Bible is His Word, it also will last forever. Our memory verse says, "Your word, O Lord, is eternal" (Ps. 119:89). Eternal is a word that means that something will never end. A Bible can become old and torn; a Bible like we carry to church can get thrown away, but the words in the Bible will never go away. The Bible will last forever because God's Word is eternal.

God gave His Word to people long ago, but He also speaks to us today through the Bible. The Bible says, "The word of God is living and active" (Heb. 4:12). It tells us how to live to please God. Once we know what is written in the Bible, we should obey it. The Bible says, "Do not merely listen to the word. . . . Do what it says" (James 1:22).

The Bible is a special book. If we do what it says, we will please God.

Activity Options

Activity 1: *Bible testimony.* Invite an older Christian to come to your classroom and talk about how God's Word has been instrumental in his or her life. Let your guest emphasize how they read the Bible everyday so that God can speak. Perhaps your visitor may have a Bible that is well used and has many markings. If so, let the children look at it and ask your guest to share some of his or her favorite underlined passages.

Activity 2: *Respecting the word.* Children can learn to respect a Bible because it is God's Word. Give the children Bibles, let them share one, or let them hold their own. Talk about how we should treat God's Word. We should be careful with its pages, not scribble in the Bible (notes and underlining are okay) or tear out pages, etc. Make sure the children understand that the book itself is not the object of our reverence but that we revere it because it contains God's message to us.

Action Point

The Bible is a special book. Will you listen when God speaks through it and do what it says?

Prayer

Dear God, thank You for giving us Your special book, the Bible. Teach us to listen to Your Word and to do what it says. Amen.

For Next Time

The Bible is God's Word and our guide. Would you like to know what else the Bible tells us? We'll find out next time.

Scripture

12 The Bible tells us about God and Jesus.

Before You Begin

- Read John 5:31–47, John 21:24–25, and Romans 15:4.
- Review the Teaching Points to familiarize yourself with the ideas to emphasize in this session.
- Read the session plan and select the elements that you will include.
- Choose a Bible memorization technique from those listed in Section 1. Be sure to vary your teaching technique from session to session.
- If you choose to include a learning activity, gather the materials you will need.
  - For Activity 1 you will need Bible and instructional books, such as a cookbook, a repair manual, or a textbook.
  - For Activity 2 you will need the open Bible pattern found on page 133.

Teaching Points

- The Bible tells us about God and Jesus.
- The Bible helps us to believe in Jesus.
- The Bible helps us to know God.

Say

What do you think the Bible is about? The Bible has a lot written in it. The Bible has stories and poetry. It tells about things that happened long ago and about things that haven't happened yet. The Bible tells about a lot of things, but everything in the Bible tells us about God and Jesus. God gave us the Bible so we could know Him. We can learn to live the way He wants us to live through Jesus.

The Bible helps us to believe in Jesus. It tells about His life on earth and all the miracles that He did. Jesus did so many things that the Bible says, "If every one of them were written down . . . the whole world would not have room for the books that would be written" (John 21:25). We don't know everything Jesus did, but knowing what Jesus did in the Bible helps us to believe in Him. The Bible says, "These are written that you may believe that Jesus is the Christ, the Son of God" (John 20:31).

When we believe in Jesus, we believe in God and we can know Him. The Bible says, "We know that we have come to know him if we obey his commands" (1 John 2:3). God's commands are written in the Bible. The Bible tells us about God and Jesus. We can learn about God and Jesus by reading the Bible. That is what the Bible is about.

Activity Options

Activity 1: *The Bible is for knowing God.* Show the children several different instructional books, such as a cookbook, a car repair manual, and a math textbook. Let the children guess what each book is for. Then talk about how people use the books to learn the subjects in them. Ask the children what book should be used to learn about God and Jesus. Show the children a Bible and talk about how knowing what the Bible says about God can help us to know Him.

Activity 2: *It's all about God.* Give each child a copy of the open Bible pattern (found in the Reproducible Activities Items section). Point out the phrase, "The Bible tells me about God and Jesus." Invite the children to make drawings of their favorite Bible stories on the pattern. Let the children tell which story their drawings represent. Talk about how the Bible has many stories and that they all tell us about God and Jesus.

Action Point

Would you like to know God and believe in Jesus? You can start by finding out what the Bible tells us about them.

Prayer

Dear God, we're glad You want us to know You. Thank You for the Bible, which tells us about You. Help us to obey all its teachings so we can believe in Jesus and know You. Amen.

For Next Time

The Bible tells us about God and Jesus, but can we believe everything the Bible says? Find out next time.

Scripture

Memory Verse
For the word of the
Lord is right and true.
Psalm 33:4

13 The stories in the Bible are true.

Before You Begin

- Read Romans 3:3–4, 2 Peter 1:16–21, and 2 Peter 3:16–18.
- Review the Teaching Points to familiarize yourself with the ideas to emphasize in this session.
- Read the session plan and select the elements that you will include.
- Choose a Bible memorization technique from those listed in Section 1. Be sure to vary your teaching technique from session to session.
- If you choose to include a learning activity, gather the materials you will need.
  - For Activity 1 you will need poster board, scissors, a ruler, a pencil, crayons, markers, stickers or other decorations, a hole punch, and yarn.

Teaching Points

- Everything in the Bible is true.
- The Bible is true even though we sometimes don't understand it.
- We cannot change truths found in the Bible.

Say

We've learned that God is good. He never does anything wrong. We've learned that the Bible is God's own Word. Since God always does right, His Word is also completely right. Everything in the Bible is true. All the stories that tell us about God and Jesus actually happened. If anyone says the Bible is not true, they are saying that God lies. The Bible says, "Let God be true, and every man a liar" (Rom. 3:4). God does not lie. All the stories in the Bible are true.

The Bible is a large book with a lot of words. Sometimes it is hard to understand everything in the Bible. The Bible says of itself that it "contains some things that are hard to understand" (2 Pet. 3:16). The Bible is true when we don't understand. We can believe what it says. We know it's true because the Bible is God's Word.

We cannot change truths found in the Bible just because we might not like what the Bible says. We must believe the Bible just the way it is. All the stories in the Bible are true and God gave them to us so that we can know Him. We must believe the Bible just as it is because it is God's Word.

Activity Options

Activity 1: *Bible bookmarks.* Before class time, cut poster board into 6"x2" strips. Make one for each child. On each strip, write, "The stories in the Bible are true." Give each child a strip to decorate as a bookmark. Let the children use crayons, markers, stickers, glitter, or whatever is available. Talk about how the Bible is full of great stories that teach us about God and, best of all, the stories are true. Punch holes in the top of the strips and tie pieces of yarn to the tops to complete the bookmarks. The children now have something to hold their place in their favorite Bible storybook.

Activity 2: *The Bible is true chorus.* Teach the children this simple chorus to the tune of "If You're Happy and You Know It.". "All the stories in the Bible are so true; All the stories in the Bible are so true; You can listen to ev'ry word and believe in all you've heard 'cause the stories in the Bible are so true!" Sing the chorus several times together.

Action Point

Have you ever wondered if all the wonderful stories in the Bible really happened? You can believe it! The stories in the Bible are true!

Prayer

Dear God, thank You for giving us a Bible full of wonderful, true stories. Help us to believe Your Word, even when we don't understand it and to never change it. It is Your Word. Amen.

For Next Time

Everything the Bible says is true, and we can believe it. But can the truth in the Bible help us know what to do? We'll find out next time.

Scripture

Memory Verse

I have hidden your word in my heart that I might not sin against you.
Psalm 119:11

14 The Bible helps me know what to do.

Before You Begin

- Read Psalm 19:7–11, Psalm 119, and Mark 4:1–20.
- Review the Teaching Points to familiarize yourself with the ideas to emphasize in this session.
- Read the session plan and select the elements that you will include.
- Choose a Bible memorization technique from those listed in Section 1. Be sure to vary your teaching technique from session to session.
- If you choose to include a learning activity, gather the materials you will need.
  - For Activity 1 you will need at least one flashlight.
  - For Activity 2 you will need one Styrofoam cup for each child, potting soil, and bean seeds.

Teaching Points

- The Bible helps me know what to do.
- The Bible is a guidebook.
- The Bible helps me follow God.
- I can hide God's Word in my heart.

Say

You make choices everyday. Some choices are small like choosing what to wear or what to eat for breakfast. Some choices are important like choosing to obey your mom and dad or choosing to tell the truth. God wants us to live the very best life possible, so He has given us the Bible to help us know what to do. The Bible asks, "How can a young person stay pure? By obeying your word and following its rules" (Ps. 119:9, NLT). The Bible is a guidebook. It can help us make right choices. The Bible helps us know what to do.

Imagine trying to walk down a path in the dark. Without a light, you wouldn't be able to see, and you would get lost. The Bible promises,

"Your word is a lamp to my feet and a light for my path" (Ps. 119:105). Just as a light would help us follow a path in the dark, the Bible will help us follow God's plan for our lives.

Have you ever planted a seed? You had to hide it in the dirt and, even though you couldn't see it, it was growing. Our memory verse says, "I have hidden your word in my heart that I might not sin against you" (Ps. 119:11). We can hide God's Word in our hearts by reading it and obeying it. If we do this, it will remind us to do right.

God gave us the Bible to help us know what to do. We can hide it in our hearts and it will show us how to follow God by doing what is right.

Activity Options

Activity 1: *The Bible is a light.* Show the children a flashlight and talk about how important it is to have light. Turn the lights off in the classroom, and show the children how dark the room is without light (cover any windows). Turn on the flashlight, and let the children use it to find their way to a designated area. Discuss how God's Word gives us light to live the way He wants us to.

Activity 2: *Plant a seed.* Give each child a cup and a bean seed. Talk about how a seed can be hidden in the soil and it will grow. Help the children scoop dirt into their cups. Help them plant the seeds and cover them in the dirt. Use this to illustrate how we can hide God's Word in our hearts just like we can hide a seed in soil. God's Word will grow in us and help us do right.

Action Point

Will you hide the words of the Bible in your heart and let them guide you? The Bible will help you know what to do.

Prayer

Dear God, thank You for giving us the Bible so we can know what to do. Help us to hide Your Word in our hearts and let it grow so we can follow You. Amen.

For Next Time

God takes great care in giving us His Word so we can know what to do. Can we really be that special to Him? Find out next time.

Self

Memory Verse
When God created people,
he made them in the
likeness of God.
Genesis 5:1, NLT

15 God made me special.

Before You Begin

- Read Genesis 1:26–27, Leviticus 20:7, Ephesians 5:1, and Philippians 2:5.
- Review the Teaching Points to familiarize yourself with the ideas to emphasize in this session.
- Read the session plan and select the elements that you will include.
- Choose a Bible memorization technique from those listed in Section 1. Be sure to vary your teaching technique from session to session.
- If you choose to include a learning activity, gather the materials you will need.
  - For Activity 1 you will need pictures of animals and people.

Teaching Points

- God made me special.
- God wants me to copy Him.
- We can be like God when we act like Jesus.

Say

Has anyone ever said you look like your mom or dad? Do you have a brother or sister who looks like you? You may look like your parents or your brothers and sisters because you are in the same family. We can't look like God but, when God made us, He made us special. The Bible says people are created, "in the likeness of God" (Gen. 5:1). We are different from animals because God made us special. God made us to be like Him.

Being like God doesn't mean that we have all power like He does. It doesn't mean that we know everything like God knows everything. Being like God means that we act like God would act and we do what God would do. "The Bible says, "Be imitators of God, therefore, as dearly loved children" (Eph. 5:1). God wants us to copy Him.

God sent His Son, Jesus, to show us how to be like God. We can be like God when we act like Jesus. The Bible says, "Your attitude should be the same as that of Christ Jesus" (Phil. 2:5). Jesus said, "I have set you an example that you should do as I have done for you" (John 13:15). When we act like Jesus, we treat others the way Jesus would treat them. We are copying God when we do that. God made us special. He made us to be like Him.

Activity Options

Activity 1: *People are special.* Show the children a variety of pictures of animals and people. Talk about how God made every living thing but He made people special. Help the children think of some ways people are different from animals. You may mention that God gave people the ability to choose and that God did not make the animals in His likeness. Emphasize that people are not animals.

Activity 2: *Imitating God.* Play a game of "copycat" with your class. Give each child a chance to be the leader, and have everyone else imitate what the leader does. Talk about ways the children can imitate God by acting like Jesus. Some ways include being kind to others, always doing what is right, and telling the truth, etc

Action Point

God made you special. He wants you to be like Him. Will you copy Jesus' example so you can be like God?

Prayer

Dear God, thank You for making us special. We want to act the way You act and do the things You do. Thank You for giving us Jesus to show us how to be like You. Amen.

For Next Time

God made us special, but do you wonder why God cares so much to make us like himself? We'll find out next time.

Self

Memory Verse
We love because he
first loved us.
1 John 4:19

16 God loves me.

Before You Begin

- Read Isaiah 43:1–5, Romans 8:37–39, and 1 John 4:7–21.
- Review the Teaching Points to familiarize yourself with the ideas to emphasize in this session.
- Read the session plan and select the elements that you will include.
- Choose a Bible memorization technique from those listed in Section 1. Be sure to vary your teaching technique from session to session.
- If you choose to include a learning activity, gather the materials you will need.
  - For Activity 1 you will need a photo of each student or a Polaroid™ camera, red construction paper with a heart shape drawn on each piece, markers, scissors, glue, and magnetic strips.

Teaching Points

- I am God's special treasure.
- Nothing can keep God from loving me.
- Because God loves me, I can love others.

Say

How do you feel when someone says to you, "I love you"? Does it make you feel special? Everyone wants to feel special, and we all need to be loved. One of the best things you can learn from the Bible is that God loves you. God calls His people "precious" (Isa. 43:4) and His "treasured possession" (Exod. 19:5). That means you are so valuable to God that you are His special treasure. God loves you.

No one loves you more than God does, and there is nothing that can keep Him from loving you. Your mom and dad love you, but God loves you more. Even when you do something that you know is bad, God still loves you. The Bible says that nothing "in all creation will ever be able to separate us from the love of God" (Rom. 8:39, NLT). He loves us no matter what.

Because God loves us, we can love others. The Bible says, "since God so loved us, we also ought to love one another" (1 John 4:11). God sent His Son, Jesus, to show us how to love others. We love others when we care about them and treat them the way Jesus would treat them. You can love others because God loves you. You are God's special treasure, and He loves you more than anyone else does. Nothing can keep Him from loving you.

Activity Options

Activity 1: *Heart magnet.* Make a reminder of God's love. If possible, obtain a photo of each of your students ahead of time, or bring a PolaroidTM camera to class to take pictures. Give each student a piece of red construction paper with a heart shape drawn on it. Let the children cut out the hearts and assist them in writing the words "God loves me" on the heart. Paste each child's photo in the center of the heart, and stick a piece of flat magnetic strip on the back. Tell the children they can put their magnets on the refrigerator or some other metal surface as a reminder that God loves them.

Activity 2: *God loves you and me.* Teach the children motions for the following two phrases. Help the class to say the sentences and make the motions together. "God" (point up toward heaven), "loves" (arms crossed in front of chest), "me" (point to yourself). In the other sentence, change the word "me" to the word "you" (point to another person); "God loves you."

Action Point

You are God's treasured possession, and we can love others because God loves us. Can you think of ways to love others?

Prayer

Dear God, thank You for loving us. Thank You that nothing can take Your love away from us. Help us to love others because You love us. Amen.

For Next Time

God loves you so much, and He wants you to have special people in your life who love you too. Who are these special people? Find out next time.

Self

Memory Verse
Children, obey your
parents in everything, for
this pleases the Lord.
Colossians 3:20

17 God made my family.

Before You Begin

- Read Proverbs 17:6, Matthew 19:13–15, Ephesians 6:1–4.
- Review the Teaching Points to familiarize yourself with the ideas to emphasize in this session.
- Read the session plan and select the elements that you will include.
- Choose a Bible memorization technique from those listed in Section 1. Be sure to vary your teaching technique from session to session.
- If you choose to include a learning activity, gather the materials you will need.
  - For Activity 1 you will need simple refreshments that are easy for young children to serve.
  - For Activity 2 you will need small branches, flowerpots or plastic cups, stones, paper strips, tape, and markers.

Teaching Points

- God made my family.
- God made my family for me.
- Families care for each other.
- I can be proud of my family.

Say

Think about your family. Maybe you have a large family with a mom, dad, and brothers and sisters. Maybe it's just you and your mom. Everyone's family is different. There are parents and grandparents, aunts and uncles, and brothers and sisters.

God made families to care for each other. God made parents to care for children by giving them food to eat and clothes to wear, to help them live a good life. The Bible tells about some parents who brought their children to Jesus. It says "little children were brought to Jesus for him to place his hands on them and pray for them" (Matt. 19:13). Those parents cared for their children by bringing them to Jesus. God wants parents to bring their children to church and to pray for them.

God gave parents for their children's own good. They look out for them by giving them rules. Our memory verse says, "Children, obey your parents in everything, for this pleases the Lord" (Col. 3:20). God is pleased when you obey your parents.

The Bible says, "parents are the pride of their children" (Prov. 17:6). You can love your family members because they are special. God made your family for you.

Activity Options

Activity 1: *Class reunion.* Give your children a chance to show off their families. Invite the parents and siblings of your students to your classroom. Let your students introduce each member of the family and tell something the family likes to do together. Let your students help serve their family members some simple refreshments. (Be sensitive to children from divorced homes or those whose parents do not attend your church.)

Activity 2: *Family trees.* Give each child a small twiggy branch, a flowerpot, or a plastic cup with the sentence "God made my family" written on it, and some stones. Help the children "plant" their twigs in the pots and surrounding them with stones so that they look like small leafless trees. Explain how a family tree shows each member of the family with the parents at the bottom and the children on the branches. Give the children strips of paper on which to write the names of family members (or they may draw family members on the strips). Use tape to attach the strips to the branch to make a family tree.

Action Point

God made your family for you. Will you remember to obey your parents? It pleases God.

Prayer

Dear God, thank You for caring enough to give us families. You made our families for our good. Help us to remember that obeying our parents pleases You. Amen.

For Next Time

God made your family for you because He loves and cares for you. How do you think we should feel toward God? We'll talk about it next time.

Self

18 God wants me to love Him.

Before You Begin

- Read Mark 12: 28–34 and John 14:21–24.
- Review the Teaching Points to familiarize yourself with the ideas to emphasize in this session.
- Read the session plan and select the elements that you will include.
- Choose a Bible memorization technique from those listed in Section 1. Be sure to vary your teaching technique from session to session.
- If you choose to include a learning activity, gather the materials you will need.
  - For Activity 1 you will need the memory verse mobile pattern found on page 134, poster board, scissors, crayons, yarn, and tape.
  - For Activity 2 you will need blank index cards, markers, stickers, and crayons.

Teaching Points

- God wants me to love Him.
- The Greatest Commandment is to love God.
- Loving God invites Him to be with me.

Say

Did you know that God wants you to love Him? God loves us, but it is also very important for us to love God. In the Bible, someone asked Jesus, "Of all the commandments, which is the most important?" (Mark 12:28) Jesus replied, "Love the Lord your God with all your heart and with all your soul and with all your mind and with all your strength" (Mark 12:30). All of God's commandments are good, and God's greatest commandment is for us to love Him. God wants you to love Him.

We are commanded to love God, but God will not make us love Him. God lets us choose. When we choose to love God, He will be near us. Jesus said, "If anyone loves me, he will obey my teaching. My Father will

46

love him, and we will come to him and make our home with him" (John 14:23). The Bible also says, "God is love. Whoever lives in love lives in God, and God in him" (1 John 4:16). We invite God to live with us if we choose to love Him.

God loves us. He wants us to love Him too. We invite Him to be with us when we choose to obey His greatest command.

Activity Options

Activity 1: *Memory verse mobile.* Ahead of time, glue copies of the memory verse mobile pattern found in the Reproducible Activities Items section to stiff poster board, and cut out the pieces. Make a set for each of your students. Let the children color the pieces. Cut varying pieces of yarn and use tape to hang the symbol pieces from the piece containing the beginning of the verse. Tape a loop of yarn to the top piece to serve as a hanger. Go over the verse with your class.

Activity 2: *Love in action.* Help children put love in action by telling others about God's love. Give each child a blank index card. Help the children to write on one side, "God loves you." On the other side write, "I love God, and I love you too!" Let the children decorate the cards with crayons and colorful stickers. Children may make as many of the cards as time allows. Encourage the children to give away their cards to others.

Action Point

God wants you to love Him. Will you choose to love Him with all your heart, soul, mind, and strength?

Prayer

Dear God, thank You for wanting our love. We want You to live in us. Help us to love You with all of our heart, soul, mind, and strength. And, as we love You, help us to love others. Amen.

For Next Time

If we love God, we will show it by loving others. Can you think of another way we might show our love for God? Find out next time.

Self

Memory Verse
This is love for God:
to obey his commands.
1 John 5:3

19 God wants me to obey him.

Before You Begin

■ Read Deuteronomy 11:1–32 and Acts 5:27–32.
■ Review the Teaching Points to familiarize yourself with the ideas to emphasize in this session.
■ Read the session plan and select the elements that you will include.
■ Choose a Bible memorization technique from those listed in Section 1. Be sure to vary your teaching technique from session to session.
■ If you choose to include a learning activity, gather the materials you will need.
  • For Activity 1 you will need a small box with a lid, a marker, a bland treat like oyster crackers, and a tasty treat like cookies or candy.
  • For Activity 2 you will need two bowls and marbles.

Teaching Points

■ God wants me to obey Him.
■ If we love God, we'll obey Him.
■ God blesses us when we obey.

Say

Do you know one of the best ways you can show love to God? The Bible gives us the answer. It says, "This is love for God: to obey His commands" (1 John 5:3). If we love God, we'll obey Him. God has always given His people good laws to help them. His commands protect us from harm and show us how to live. God tells us what to do because He loves us and, if we love God, we'll do what He says. God wants you to obey Him.

God wants us to have everything we need, and His commands are for our good. In the Bible, God's people were about to enter the land that God was giving them. God told them about all the good things that they would have if they did what He commanded. He reminded them, "be sure that you obey all the decrees and laws I am setting before you today" (Deut. 11:32). God blesses us when we obey.

Activity Options

Activity 1: *Obedience box.* Put a bland snack in a box with a lid. Write on the box: Do not open! Hide a better treat out of sight. Discuss what might be in the box and what might happen if it is opened. Let the class choose whether to open the box or to leave the box alone. If the box is opened, serve the treat it contains, but show the treat the class missed. If the class obeys, serve the good treat. Show what was in the other box, and talk about how obeying God's commands are best.

Activity 2: *Fully obey.* Show the children two bowls, one empty and one filled with marbles. Suppose God's command was to transfer all the marbles from one bowl to the other. Talk about how not doing it at all is disobedience. Transfer some of the marbles. Ask the children if this is obedience. Transfer all the marbles except one. Use this object lesson to demonstrate that we are not fully obeying God until we do completely what He says.

Action Point

God wants to bless us, but we must always do what He says. Do you love God? If you do, you'll obey Him.

Prayer

Dear God, thank You that you give us commands because You love us. Help us to obey You even when it's hard. We want to obey you because we love you. Amen.

For Next Time

God wants you to obey Him, but how can you know what's right and what's wrong? We'll talk about it next time.

Self

Memory Verse
Righteous are you, O Lord,
and your laws are right.
Psalm 119:137

20   I can know right from wrong.

Before You Begin

- Read Genesis 4:6–7, Proverbs 2, and Proverbs 14:12.
- Review the Teaching Points to familiarize yourself with the ideas to emphasize in this session.
- Read the session plan and select the elements that you will include.
- Choose a Bible memorization technique from those listed in Section 1. Be sure to vary your teaching technique from session to session.
- If you choose to include a learning activity, gather the materials you will need.
  - For Activity 2 you will need red and green paper, a marker, tape, and a Bible.

Teaching Points

- I can know right from wrong.
- The Bible shows us right from wrong.
- God decides what is right.
- God warns us when we do wrong.

Say

We've already learned that God loves us. He gives us good rules, and He wants us to obey His commands. God wants us to do what is right, but we don't have to guess how. We can know right from wrong because God shows us right from wrong in the Bible. The Bible says, "Righteous are you, O Lord, and your laws are right" (Ps. 119:137). As we learn God's commands, we learn what is right.

God tells us the difference between right and wrong. The Bible says, "There is a way that seems right to a man, but in the end it leads to death" (Prov. 14:12). God decides what is right, and we need Him to teach us. The Bible encourages us to learn God's wisdom and says that when we do, we will "understand what is right and just" (Prov. 2:9).

Have you ever felt bad for doing something that you know is wrong? That bad feeling is called guilt. God warns us when we do wrong. He lets us feel guilty so we will stop doing wrong and do right. In the Bible, when the people of Israel were guilty of doing wrong, God told them, "Stop doing wrong, learn to do right!" (Isa. 1:16–17).

You and I can stop doing wrong and learn to do right too. We can learn what God says in the Bible. Then we can know right from wrong.

Activity Options

Activity 1: *Three ways to know.* Teach your class three ways to know right from wrong. Have the children hold their hands like an open book, representing the Bible. Say, "The Bible shows us right from wrong." Then have the children lay their hands on their hearts. Say, "We should not do something that makes us feel guilty." Have the children raise a hand. Tell the children, "When you are not sure what's right or wrong, you can ask your parents, Sunday school teacher, or pastor." Help the children recite these three methods of knowing right from wrong.

Activity 2: *Right or wrong*? Encourage the children that they are already learning right from wrong. On a green sheet of paper, write the word "right." Write the word "wrong" on a red sheet. Tape the papers to opposite walls. Have the children go to the sign that shows if these statements are right or wrong: Obey your parents. Take something that is not yours. Obey God. Be mean to others. You may think of others as time allows.

Action Point

Will you remember to stop doing wrong and learn to do right? The Bible can show you right from wrong.

Prayer

Dear God, thank You for Your Word that shows us right from wrong. Thank You for guilty feelings that help us to know when we've done wrong. Help us to do what the Bible says because it is right. Amen.

For Next Time

We can know right from wrong through God's Word, the Bible. God also gave us someone special to teach us. Do you know who He is? Find out next time.

Jesus

Memory Verse
Who is it that overcomes
the world? Only he who believes
that Jesus is the Son of God.
1 John 5:5

21 Jesus is God's son.

Before You Begin

- Read John 1:1–18, Hebrews 1:1–14, and 1 John 5:1–12.
- Review the Teaching Points to familiarize yourself with the ideas to emphasize in this session.
- Read the session plan and select the elements that you will include.
- Choose a Bible memorization technique from those listed in Section 1. Be sure to vary your teaching technique from session to session.
- If you choose to include a learning activity, gather the materials you will need.
  - For Activity 1 you will need the God's Son puzzle pattern and picture of Jesus found on pages 135 and 136, tape, and crayons.
  - For Activity 2 you will need index cards, a marker, pencils, one large ball, and one small ball.

Teaching Points

- Jesus is God's Son.
- Jesus is equal with God.
- We must obey Jesus.

Say

Can you think of something that you learned to do because your mom or dad showed you how to do it? It's easy to learn something when we have someone to show us how it is done. God wants us to know Him and to learn what He is like. He gives us His Son, Jesus, as an example. Jesus is God's Son. He shows us what God is like. In the Bible, Jesus says, "Anyone who has seen me has seen the Father" (John 14:9). When we look at Jesus, we learn what God is like because Jesus is God's Son.

Jesus is equal with God, and He has always existed. Just like God, the Father, He has no beginning. The Bible says, "He was with God in the beginning" (John 1:2). Jesus helped make the world. The Bible says, "Through him all things were made" (John 1:3). Jesus is equal with God. He is God, the Son.

If we want to follow the example God has given us, we must love and obey His Son, Jesus. The Bible says, "If anyone says that Jesus is the Son of God, God lives in him and he in God" (1 John 4:15). We cannot know God if we do not accept Jesus. Jesus is equal with God. He shows us what God is like. If we want to love and obey God, we must love and obey Jesus because Jesus is God's Son.

Activity Options

Activity 1: *God's Son puzzle.* Make each student a copy of the puzzle found on pages 135–136 with the puzzle pattern on one side and the picture of Jesus on the other. Cut the pieces ahead of time. Have the children put the puzzle together using the side with the words, "God's Son?" Tape the completed puzzles together. Turn the puzzles over to reveal the picture of Jesus. Let the children color the picture of Jesus.

Activity 2: *Greater or equal?* Show the children an index card with the symbol > drawn on it. Demonstrate how the symbol works. Place the card between two balls, one larger or greater than the other one. Another example is one pencil is less than three pencils. Then show an index card with an equal sign drawn it. Demonstrate that symbol; one pencil is equal to one pencil. Write the following words on index cards: God, Jesus, the world, people. Help the children arrange the cards around the symbols to discuss these statements: God > the world. God > people. Jesus > the world. Jesus > people. Jesus = God.

Action Point

Do you believe that Jesus is God's Son? If so, remember to love and obey Him because Jesus is equal with God.

Prayer

Dear God, we believe that Jesus is Your Son. Thank You for sending Jesus to be our example. Help us to love and obey Him because when we do, we love and obey You too. Amen.

For Next Time

Jesus is God's Son and He has always existed, but did you know Jesus came to earth as a little baby? We'll talk about that next time.

Jesus

Memory Verse
For to us a child is born,
to us a son is given.
Isaiah 9:6

22 Jesus was born as a baby.

Before You Begin

- Read Isaiah 9:2–7 and Luke 2:1–20.
- Review the Teaching Points to familiarize yourself with the ideas to emphasize in this session.
- Read the session plan and select the elements that you will include.
- Choose a Bible memorization technique from those listed in Section 1. Be sure to vary your teaching technique from session to session.
- If you choose to include a learning activity, gather the materials you will need.
  - For Activity 1 you will need a Christmas nativity scene.
  - For Activity 2 you will need a picture of Jesus as a baby, a nativity figurine, or an index card with Jesus' name written on it. Also, you will need a box to be wrapped as a gift and any items used to celebrate a birthday.

Teaching Points

- Jesus was born as a baby.
- Jesus' birth is good news for everyone.
- Jesus is our gift from God.

Say

Do you like to celebrate Christmas? We decorate our houses, and we gather with our families. We sing special songs. Christmas is special because we celebrate Jesus' birth. Jesus was born as a baby. When God sent His Son into the world, He chose to come in this way. God told a young girl named Mary that she would be Jesus' mother. He sent an angel to tell her, "You will be with child and give birth to a son, and you are to give him the name Jesus" (Luke 1:31).

When Jesus was born, it was good news. The Bible tells about the angels in heaven celebrating and spreading the message that Jesus was born. They said to some shepherds, "I bring you good news of great joy that will be for all the people. Today in the town of David a Savior has been born to you; he is Christ the Lord" (Luke 2:10–11). Jesus came to be our Savior and to help us. Jesus' birth is good news for everyone.

Jesus is our gift from God. God planned to give us His Son from the very beginning. Long before Jesus was born, the Bible talks about God's gift. It says, "For to us a child is born, to us a son is given" (Isa. 9:6). God gave His Son to help us know how to be like Him. Jesus was born as a baby, and His coming is good news to us all.

Activity Options

Activity 1: *Christmas story.* Show the children a nativity scene. Let the children take turns putting the pieces of the scene in the proper places as you briefly tell the Christmas story. Remind the children that even when Jesus came as a baby, He was still God.

Activity 2: *Birthday party.* Ahead of time, place a picture of Jesus as baby, a nativity scene figurine of Jesus, or even an index card with Jesus' name on it in a box. Wrap the box as a gift. Have a birthday party for Jesus. Serve birthday cake or another kind of treat. Lead the children in singing "Happy Birthday" to Jesus. Show the children the gift. Talk about how it's fun to receive gifts when it's our birthday. When it was Jesus' birthday, He gave us a gift instead. Let the children unwrap the gift. Remove the item representing Jesus to show that Jesus gave us himself.

Action Point

Jesus was born as a baby. Did you know that He came as a gift for you? That is good news.

Prayer

Dear God, thank You for Jesus. We are glad that He was born to be a gift for us. That is good news! Help us to accept Your gift by letting Jesus teach us how to be like You. Amen.

For Next Time

Jesus was born as a baby, but He did not stay a baby. Just like you, He grew up. Let's talk about it next time.

Jesus

Memory Verse
So Jesus grew both in height and in wisdom, and he was loved by God and by all who knew him.
Luke 2:52, NLT

23 Jesus grew up, just like me.

Before You Begin

- Read Isaiah 11:1–3, Isaiah 53:1–2, and Luke 2:39–52.
- Review the Teaching Points to familiarize yourself with the ideas to emphasize in this session.
- Read the session plan and select the elements that you will include.
- Choose a Bible memorization technique from those listed in Section 1. Be sure to vary your teaching technique from session to session.
- If you choose to include a learning activity, gather the materials you will need.
  - For Activity 1 you will need baby pictures of your students, a measuring stick or tape, and tape.
  - For Activity 2 you will need a ball.

Teaching Points

- Jesus grew like every baby does.
- Jesus loved and obeyed His Heavenly Father.
- Jesus obeyed His parents.

Say

Do you look different now than when you were a baby? Of course you do! You are taller. You can walk and talk and feed yourself. Like all babies, you grew up, and you are still growing. Jesus was born a baby and, just like you, He grew up. He got taller, and he learned to walk and talk and eat on His own. Jesus is God's Son, but because He chose to come as a baby, He grew like every baby does.

The Bible says, "So Jesus grew both in height and in wisdom, and he was loved by God and by all who knew him" (Luke 2:52, NLT). Growing in wisdom means Jesus learned how to do some things just like you. Growing in height means Jesus got taller and stronger, just like you too.

Jesus also grew in favor with God. That means He loved and obeyed His Heavenly Father, and God was pleased with Him. God would later say of Jesus, "This is my Son, whom I love; with him I am well pleased" (Matt. 3:17).

Everyone likes a child who is kind and obedient. The Bible says Jesus was loved by all who knew Him. That means He pleased other people by the way He behaved. Jesus had parents just like you, and He always obeyed them. The Bible says he "was obedient to them" (Luke 2:51).

Jesus grew up, just like you. You can grow up just like Jesus, learning things, getting taller and stronger, and pleasing God and others.

Activity Options

Activity 1: *Measure up!* Show your class how they've grown. If possible, arrange to have baby pictures of your students. Talk about how everyone has grown. Use a measuring stick or tape to measure how tall each student is. Use a piece of tape to mark everyone's height on the wall. Remind the children that Jesus was once a baby too. He grew up just like the children are growing now.

Activity 2: *Play a game.* When Jesus was a child, He probably liked to play games. Play this game with your class. Have everyone stand in circle. To start the game, say, "Jesus grew up like you and me. Do you think He liked to play ball?" Let the children toss or pass a ball around the circle until you tell them to stop. Whoever is holding the ball must repeat the phrase, changing the game or activity to something they like to do. Start the ball again. The child that just spoke gets to be the one to tell the others to stop. Let everyone have at least one turn.

Action Point

Can you please God and others by the way you behave? If so, you'll grow up like Jesus did.

Prayer

Dear God, thank You for helping us to grow up. Thank You that we can learn things and that we can grow strong and tall. Help each child here to grow like Jesus, pleasing You and others. Amen.

For Next Time

We've learned that Jesus grew up, obeying His parents and pleasing God. Do you think it's possible that Jesus always obeyed God? We'll find out.

Jesus

24 Jesus always obeyed God.

Before You Begin

- Read John 5:16–30 and Philippians 2:5–11.
- Review the Teaching Points to familiarize yourself with the ideas to emphasize in this session.
- Read the session plan and select the elements that you will include.
- Choose a Bible memorization technique from those listed in Section 1. Be sure to vary your teaching technique from session to session.
- If you choose to include a learning activity, gather the materials you will need.
  - For Activity 2 you will need the clock pattern found on page 137, scissors, brass fasteners, and crayons.

Teaching Points

- Jesus always obeyed God.
- Jesus came to do God's will.
- Jesus said what God wanted Him to say.
- Jesus obeyed God out of love.

Say

Did you know that Jesus didn't do just what He wanted to do? Jesus came to do what God wanted. God sent His Son, Jesus, to show us what God is like. God sent Jesus to help us. Jesus came to do God's will. Jesus said, "For I have come down from heaven not to do my will but to do the will of him who sent me" (John 6:38). Jesus came to earth because God sent Him. He came to do what God wanted Him to do. Jesus always obeyed God.

Jesus said what God wanted Him to say no matter what others thought. Sometimes Jesus said things that made some people mad. They were mad because they were doing bad things that Jesus said they shouldn't do. Some people wondered how Jesus knew so much. The Bible says,

58

"Jesus answered, 'My teaching is not my own. It comes from him who sent me'" (John 7:16).

Have you ever had to do something you didn't want to do? Maybe your parents told you to do something you didn't want to do, but you obeyed them because you love them. Jesus obeyed God out of love. Jesus had a very hard thing to do that we'll learn about later, but He did it because He loved His Heavenly Father. He said, "The world must learn that I love the Father and that I do exactly what my Father has commanded me" (John 14:31). Jesus always obeyed God.

Activity Options

Activity 1: *Obeying game.* Play this game as you would play "Simon Says." Tell the class they are going to play "Teacher Says." Tell the children to listen closely while you give them simple commands that are easy to follow. The children are only to obey the ones that begin with "Teacher says." Talk about how Jesus always obeyed God, no matter He said. We can obey God too if we do what He wants us to do.

Activity 2: *All the time.* Give each child a copy of the clock pattern found in the Reproducible Activities Items section. Have the children cut out the clock shape and the hands. Color the clock with crayons. Use a brass fastener to attach the hands to the clock face. Read the words on the clock to your class, "Jesus always obeyed God. I can obey God at all times." Talk about how there is never a time we shouldn't obey God.

Action Point

Jesus always obeyed God because He loved His Heavenly Father. Do you love God enough to always obey Him?

Prayer

Dear God, thank You for sending Jesus to help us. We're glad that He always obeyed You. Help us to be like Jesus and love You so much that we always obey You too. Amen.

For Next Time

Jesus always obeyed God, and everything He said and did taught the people about somebody. Can you guess who it was? We'll find out.

Jesus

25 Jesus taught people about God.

Before You Begin

- Read Matthew 5–7, Luke 15:11–31, and John 1:18.
- Review the Teaching Points to familiarize yourself with the ideas to emphasize in this session.
- Read the session plan and select the elements that you will include.
- Choose a Bible memorization technique from those listed in Section 1. Be sure to vary your teaching technique from session to session.
- If you choose to include a learning activity, gather the materials you will need.
  - For Activity 1 you will need the "Who teaches?" worksheet found on page 138, and crayons.
  - For Activity 2 you will need a Bible storybook, and a guest story-teller (optional).

Teaching Points

- Jesus was a teacher.
- Jesus taught people about God.
- We learn about God when we see how Jesus lived.

Say

What does a teacher do? They teach, of course! They tell us about things or show us how to do things. Did you know that Jesus was a teacher too? The people often called Him "Teacher." What do you think Jesus taught? Jesus taught the people about God.

If you wanted to learn to play the piano, who would be the best teacher—someone who actually plays the piano or someone who's just read about it? The person who knows how to play would be the best teacher. Teachers teach what they know. A math teacher teaches about math. A music teacher teaches about music. There is no one who can teach about God as well as Jesus can. When Jesus taught the people, the Bible says, "The crowds were amazed at his teaching, because he taught as one who had authority" (Matt. 7:28–29). Jesus had a right to teach about God because He was God's Son.

Jesus teaches us about God. We learn about God when we see how Jesus lived. Jesus said, "Anyone who has seen me has seen the Father" (John 14:9). We can't see Jesus with our eyes, but the Bible helps us see how He lived His life on earth. If we want to learn about God, Jesus is our expert teacher. He teaches people about God and is an example of what God is like.

Activity Options

Activity 1: *Who teaches?* Give each child a copy of the "Who Teaches?" worksheet found in the Reproducible Activities Items section. Show the children how to draw a line to connect each teacher with the subject they teach. Talk about how, as God's Son, Jesus is the best teacher to teach people about God.

Activity 2: *Parables.* One of the ways Jesus taught the people was to tell parables. Explain to the children that a parable is a story about common things that has a heavenly meaning. Tell the parable of the prodigal son to your class. You may wish to read it from a Bible storybook or even have a guest storyteller tell the story. Tell the students that this was a story that Jesus told, and lead the children in understanding how this story demonstrates what God the Father is like.

Action Point

Jesus taught people about God because He had the authority to do so. Are you willing to learn what God is like from Jesus' example?

Prayer

Dear God, thank You for Jesus and that He can teach us about You. Help us to learn from His example so that we can do what pleases You. Amen.

For Next Time

Jesus taught the people about God, and He gives us an example of what God is like. Why do you suppose Jesus does all of this for us? We'll find out.

Jesus

Memory Verse
As the Father has loved me,
so have I loved you.
Now remain in my love.
John 15:9

26 Jesus loves me.

Before You Begin

- Read John 15:9–17, Ephesians 5:1–2, and Revelation 3:9.
- Review the Teaching Points to familiarize yourself with the ideas to emphasize in this session.
- Read the session plan and select the elements that you will include.
- Choose a Bible memorization technique from those listed in Section 1. Be sure to vary your teaching technique from session to session.
- If you choose to include a learning activity, gather the materials you will need.
  - For Activity 1 you will need the "Giving Certificate" found on page 139, pencils, and crayons.
  - For Activity 2 you will need drawing paper, markers, alphabet stencils, and adhesive letters or cutouts.

Teaching Points

- Jesus loves you.
- Jesus gives himself to us out of love.
- Others see how Jesus loves us.

Say

The Bible says Jesus "went around doing good" (Acts 10:38). He made blind people see and crippled people walk. He fed the hungry and taught the people about God. Do you know why Jesus did good deeds? It is because He loved the people.

And Jesus loves you! In the Bible, Jesus said to His followers, "As the Father loves me, so have I loved you" (John 15:9). Imagine that! Jesus loves you like God loves Him.

When you love others, you want to be with them. You want to do nice things for them. When you love others, you want to give yourself to them. Because Jesus loves us, He wants to be with us and do things for us. Jesus gives himself to us out of love. The Bible says, "Christ loved us and gave himself up for us" (Eph. 5:2). Jesus gives himself to you.

When we really believe Jesus loves us, it makes a difference in how we act and what we do. Jesus says to us, "Love each other as I have loved you" (John 15:12). When we love others as Jesus loves us, people notice. When others see how Jesus loves us, they may let Jesus love them too. Jesus loves you!

Activity Options

Activity 1: *Give yourself.* Help the children give of themselves as Jesus gives of himself. Give each child a copy of the "Giving Certificate" found in the Reproducible Activities Items section. Talk about how Jesus was kind to people because He loved them. Ask the children to think of someone they love, and help them to write that person's name in the space provided. Have the children think of something that they can do to show love for that person. Ideas can range from doing a chore for a parent without being asked to giving a hug to someone. Help the children write their ideas in the space provided. Decorate the certificate with crayons. Children should give the certificate to the person they named and do the activity they chose.

Activity 2: *Make it personal.* Give each child a sheet of drawing paper with the words "Jesus loves" written at the top. Have the children use alphabet stencils, adhesive letters, or cutouts to make their names under the phrase. Talk about how Jesus loves each child personally.

Action Point

Jesus loves you and wants to give himself to you. When others look at you, will they be able to see how Jesus loves you?

Prayer

Dear Jesus, thank You for loving us and for giving Yourself to us. We want to love You. Help us to love others so that they will see Your love for us and know that You love them too. Amen.

For Next Time

Jesus loves us so much that He did a very hard thing for us that we couldn't do for ourselves. We'll talk about it next time.

Jesus

27 Jesus died on the cross.

Before You Begin

- Read John 19:1–42, Romans 6:19–23, and Hebrews 9:11–10:18.
- Review the Teaching Points to familiarize yourself with the ideas to emphasize in this session.
- Read the session plan and select the elements that you will include.
- Choose a Bible memorization technique from those listed in Section 1. Be sure to vary your teaching technique from session to session.
- If you choose to include a learning activity, gather the materials you will need.
  - For Activity 1 you will need a dollar bill or coins, and a box wrapped like a gift.
  - For Activity 2 you will need a Bible storybook with a picture of the crucifixion, two dowel rods for each child (one six inches long and the other three inches long), a hot glue gun, small strips of poster board, markers, and glue.

Teaching Points

- Death is the payment for sin.
- Jesus died on the cross to pay for sin.
- Jesus gave His life.

Say

Have you ever done something to earn payment? Some children get things for doing chores around the house. Grownups work to earn money. When someone earns something for what they do, we call what they earn "wages."

Our memory verse talks about wages too. It says, "the wages of sin is death" (Rom. 6:23). Did you know people could earn death by disobeying God? It's true. As bad as that sounds, the Bible says the payment for sin is death.

It is one of God's rules that sin earns death. God doesn't want anyone to die, so He sent someone to take the payment for sin. Our memory verse says, "the gift of God is eternal life in Christ Jesus our Lord" (Rom. 6:23). God gave us His Son. Jesus died on the cross to pay for our sin.

Jesus let people hang Him on a cross. He hung on the cross until He died because of sin, but Jesus never did any wrong. He didn't have to die and nobody made Him do it. Jesus gave His life one time to pay for everyone's sin. The Bible says, "Christ died for sins once for all" (1 Pet. 3:18).

Jesus died on the cross. He paid the full price of sin. Because He died, God can offer us the gift of eternal life instead of the wages of sin.

Activity Options

Activity 1: *Gift or wages.* Show the class a dollar or some coins, and a brightly wrapped package. Explain the difference between earning wages and receiving a gift. Explain that when someone works for wages, they get what they earn. Sin earns us death. Explain that you can't earn a gift. A gift is given. Remind the children that Jesus died on the cross to pay for sin so that we could be given the gift of eternal life.

Activity 2: *The cross.* Using a Bible storybook, show the class a picture of the crucifixion. Help the children understand that Jesus hung on a cross to die. Give each child two dowel rods—one that is six inches long and one that is three inches long. Use a hot glue gun to glue the pieces together to form a cross. You should operate the hot glue, and let the child lay the short stick on the bead of glue. Write, "Jesus died on the cross" on a strip of poster board. Children may use white glue to stick this on the cross.

Action Point

Jesus died on the cross even though He never sinned. What have your actions been earning you?

Prayer

Dear Jesus, thank You for dying on the cross. We're glad that You gave Your life to make the payment for sin so we could have eternal life. Help us to accept Your gift. Amen.

For Next Time

Jesus died on the cross to pay for every sin, but that is not the end. Jesus is alive! We'll find out more next time.

Jesus

Memory Verse
He is not here; he
has risen, just as he said.
Matthew 28:6

28 Jesus is alive.

Before You Begin

- Read Matthew 28:1–10, John 20:1–18, and Acts 2:22–36.
- Review the Teaching Points to familiarize yourself with the ideas to emphasize in this session.
- Read the session plan and select the elements that you will include.
- Choose a Bible memorization technique from those listed in Section 1. Be sure to vary your teaching technique from session to session.
- If you choose to include a learning activity, gather the materials you will need.
  - For Activity 1 you will need crayons and the empty tomb pattern found on page 140.

Teaching Point

- Jesus became alive again.
- People saw Jesus alive.
- Jesus went into Heaven.

Say

When Jesus died on the cross, His body was placed in a tomb. But did you know Jesus did not stay there? The Bible says, "God raised him from the dead . . . because it was impossible for death to keep its hold on him" (Acts 2:24). Jesus became alive again! Only God can do a miracle like that. We celebrate the miracle of Jesus rising from the dead on Easter Sunday.

The Bible says people saw Jesus alive. Some women went to see where Jesus was buried, but when they got there, they found the stone rolled away and an angel there. The angel said to the women, "Do not be afraid, for I know that you are looking for Jesus, who was crucified. He is not here; he has risen, just as he said" (Matt. 28:5–6). Jesus told His followers He would rise again, and it was true. Many of them saw Jesus die, and they saw Him alive again.

After people saw Jesus alive, He went up into heaven. The Bible says, "He was taken up into heaven and he sat at the right hand of God" (Mark 16:19). Jesus said, "I am going there to prepare a place for you" (John 14:2). Jesus wants us to have a place in heaven too. That is why He died. Jesus rose from the dead and is alive today. He is in heaven with God, preparing a place for you and me.

Activity Options

Activity 1: *Empty tomb.* Prepare for each child a copy of the empty tomb pattern (found in the Reproducible Activities Items section) according to the directions. Let the children color the tomb and the stone. Slide the paper handle through the slots so the stone covers the tomb door. Show the children how to slide the stone back to reveal the memory verse underneath.

Activity 2: *He is risen.* Teach your class the phrase, "He is risen" and the answering phrase, "He is risen, indeed." Explain that indeed is a word that describes something as being absolutely true without question. The fact that Jesus is alive is absolutely true and without question. Divide the class into two groups and place them on opposite sides of the room. Have one group say, "He is risen" and the other group answer, "He is risen, indeed." Then have the group switch the phrases and say them again.

Action Point

Jesus died and rose again. He is alive in heaven. Do you believe He is preparing a place for you?

Prayer

Dear Jesus, we rejoice that You are alive today. Thank You for preparing a place in heaven for us. Help us to live the way You want us to so that we can be with You. Amen.

For Next Time

Jesus is alive, but what is so bad about sin that Jesus had to die because of it? We'll talk about it next time.

Salvation

29 There is one true God.

Before You Begin

- Read Genesis 3:1–24 and Romans 7:7–12.
- Review the Teaching Points to familiarize yourself with the ideas to emphasize in this session.
- Read the session plan and select the elements that you will include.
- Choose a Bible memorization technique from those listed in Section 1. Be sure to vary your teaching technique from session to session.
- If you choose to include a learning activity, gather the materials you will need.
  - For Activity 1 you will need paper and markers.

Teaching Points

- Sin is doing wrong.
- Sin is not doing what we know we should.
- Sin is disobeying God.

Say

Have you ever done something bad—something you knew was wrong but did anyway? We've all done bad things. When we do something we know is wrong, it is called sin. The Bible says, "All wrongdoing is sin" (1 John 5:17). "Wrongdoing" is doing wrong, and sin is doing wrong.

Sin is not just doing wrong. If we know something good that we ought to do, and we do not do it, that is sin too. The Bible says, "Anyone, then, who knows the good he ought to do and doesn't do it, sins" (James 4:17). Sin is not doing what we know we should.

God's law tells us what is right and wrong. He gives us His law so we will know what sin is. In the Bible, one of Jesus' followers named Paul wrote, "Indeed I would not have known what sin was except through

68

the law" (Rom. 7:7). We have learned that we should always obey God's rules. When we disobey them, we sin. Sin is disobeying God.

Sin is not making a mistake. A mistake is something we don't mean to do, but sin is something we do on purpose. Sin is disobeying God by doing something He says we should not do. Sin is also not doing something we know we should do. Sin is doing wrong.

Activity Options

Activity 1: *When we know.* Place sheets of paper in a circle on the floor. Write on one piece: "Do not step on this paper!" Put that paper, written side down, among the others. Have the children walk on the paper circle. Then, show the children the paper with the rule. Talk about how they could not have known about the rule. Return the paper to the circle, with the written side up. Stepping on that paper now would be wrong because we know we shouldn't do it. Talk about how God's law shows us what sin is.

Activity 2: *Sin or mistake?* Read the following scenario several times: "Billy's parents told him not to run in the house or he might break something." Each time you read it, change the ending: "Billy ran anyway and broke a vase." "Billy walked and nothing got broken." "Billy ran anyway, but his parents never knew." "Billy accidentally bumped into the vase and broke it." Talk about each ending and about the difference between sin and mistakes.

Action Point

Have you ever done something you knew was wrong, or have you ever not done something you knew you should? If so, it is sin.

Prayer

Dear God, Thank You for showing us what sin is. Help us to always do what we ought to do and never do what we know is wrong so that we never disobey You. Amen.

For Next Time

Sin is doing wrong, and we sin when we disobey God. Who do you think has disobeyed God? Find out next time.

Salvation

30 Everyone has disobeyed God.

Before You Begin

- Read Genesis 3:1–24, Jeremiah 2:22, Romans 5:12–14, and 1 John 1:8, 10.
- Review the Teaching Points to familiarize yourself with the ideas to emphasize in this session.
- Read the session plan and select the elements that you will include.
- Choose a Bible memorization technique from those listed in Section 1. Be sure to vary your teaching technique from session to session.
- If you choose to include a learning activity, gather the materials you will need.
  - For Activity 1 you will need paper, markers, and beanbags.
  - For Activity 2 you will need a handkerchief, food coloring, and a large bowl of water.

Teaching Points

- Everyone has disobeyed God.
- We can choose to obey God, or we can choose to sin.
- Everyone has sinned.

Say

We know that disobeying God is sin. But did you know God lets people choose whether or not they will obey Him? God gave the first people, Adam and Eve, that choice. They could choose to obey God or sin against Him by not obeying. Adam and Eve chose to disobey God, and their choice brought sin into the world. Adam and Eve's sin makes people more likely to choose sin over obedience. The Bible says, "Through the disobedience of the one man the many were made sinners" (Rom. 5:19). We can choose to obey God or choose to sin.

Sadly, the Bible says everyone has chosen to disobey. It says, "For all have sinned and fall short of the glory of God" (Rom. 3:23). To fall short means we disobey God and can't measure up to what God planned for us. Everyone has sinned. Everyone includes you and me.

Have you ever had a stain on your clothes that wouldn't come out, even after it had been washed? Sin leaves a stain on our lives, and there is nothing we can do to get rid of it. When the people of Israel disobeyed God, He said to them, "Although you wash yourself . . . and use an abundance of soap, the stain of your guilt is still before me" (Jer. 2:22). God sees the stain sin makes on our lives.

Disobeying God is sin. Everyone has disobeyed God. Everyone has sinned.

Activity Options

Activity 1: *Falling short of God's glory.* You'll need to use the church's fellowship hall or parking lot for this activity. Write the words "God's Love," "God's Patience," "God's Goodness," and "God's Wisdom" on several sheets of paper. Place them face up as far away from the children as possible. Give the children beanbags and have them take turns tossing the beanbags at the papers, which should be out of their range. Use this activity to demonstrate how we fall short of God's plan for us. It's impossible for us to live as God planned without His help.

Activity 2: *Sin's stain.* Show the children a clean white handkerchief. Explain that sin leaves a stain on our hearts that we can't get rid of. Allow the children to take turns putting drops of food coloring on the handkerchief. Place the handkerchief in a bowl of water or in a sink to demonstrate that the stains can't be washed away. Talk about how sin leaves a stain on our hearts that we can't get rid of.

Action Point

Everyone has disobeyed God. Do you know what things you have done to disobey God? Remember that disobeying God is sin.

Prayer

Dear God, thank You that we can choose to obey You. Help us to never choose sin. We are sorry that we've disobeyed You and have fallen short of Your glory. Help us to always choose to obey. Amen.

For Next Time

Everyone has disobeyed God, including you and me. Because of sin, how do you think God feels toward us? We'll talk about it next time.

Salvation

31 God wants to forgive me.

Before You Begin

- Read Isaiah 1:18 and 55:6–7, Micah 7:18–20, and 1 John 1:9.
- Review the Teaching Points to familiarize yourself with the ideas to emphasize in this session.
- Read the session plan and select the elements that you will include.
- Choose a Bible memorization technique from those listed in Section 1. Be sure to vary your teaching technique from session to session.
- If you choose to include a learning activity, gather the materials you will need.
  - For Activity 1 you will need the "New Words" symbols found on page 142.
  - For Activity 2 you will need crayons and the "Make It Personal" pattern found on page 141.

Teaching Points

- God wants to forgive us.
- We must tell God what we have done.
- We must stop doing wrong.

Say

If you do something wrong to someone else, what do your parents tell you to do? They will want you to say, "I'm sorry." They will want you to ask that person to forgive you for doing wrong. To forgive someone means to not hold that thing against that person. You may still be hurt or angry, but you don't want to hurt or hate that person because of what they did to you. The Bible tells us that we have sinned against God. We have done wrong. We deserve for God to be angry with us, but the Bible tells us God wants to forgive us. The Bible says, "If we confess our sins, he is faithful and just and will forgive us our sins" (1 John 1:9). To confess means to admit to God that we have sinned.

God wants us to be honest about our sin. We must tell God what we have done. In the Bible, David said about God, "'I will confess my transgressions to the Lord'—and you forgave the guilt of my sin" (Ps. 32:5). We can tell God what we've done, and He will forgive us.

If we want God's forgiveness, we must repent. Repent means to stop sinning. It means we decide we never want to do that sin again. The Bible says, "Repent, then, and turn to God, so that your sins may be wiped out" (Acts 3:19). We must stop doing wrong.

God wants to forgive us. If we confess our sins to Him and decide to stop doing wrong, He will forgive us.

Activity Options

Activity 1: *New words.* Use the "New Words" symbols found in the Reproducible Activities Items section to help your class understand the words "confess" and "repent." Show the children the picture of someone talking and remind the class that to confess means to admit to God that we have sinned, to tell Him what we have done. Show the children the stop sign symbol. Explain that the word repent means that we decide to stop doing whatever sin we've been practicing. Explain that doing these two things is very important when we want God to forgive us.

Activity 2: *Make it personal.* Give each child a copy of the "Make It Personal" pattern found in the Reproducible Activities Items section. Read the concept, "God wants to forgive . . . " aloud, and encourage the children to write their names in the space provided. Let the children color the pattern. Help the children read the concept with their name added so that they understand that God wants to forgive them.

Action Point

Did you know God wants you to confess your sins and choose to live for Him? God wants to forgive you. Why not confess to Him today?

Prayer

Dear God, thank You that You will forgive us if we sin. Help us to come to You when we do wrong and to be honest about what we've done. Help us to choose You over sin. Amen.

For Next Time

God wants to forgive us, but sin must also be punished. Do you know who took the punishment for your sins? We'll talk about it next time.

Salvation

32 Jesus died for my sin.

Before You Begin

- Read Isaiah 53, John 3:16–18, and Romans 5:6–11.
- Review the Teaching Points to familiarize yourself with the ideas to emphasize in this session.
- Read the session plan and select the elements that you will include.
- Choose a Bible memorization technique from those listed in Section 1. Be sure to vary your teaching technique from session to session.
- If you choose to include a learning activity, gather the materials you will need.
  - For Activity 1 you will need a large glass bowl, food coloring, bleach, and the handkerchief from the previous lesson (optional).
  - For Activity 2 you will need the "More Words" symbols found on page 143.

Teaching Points

- Jesus died for your sin.
- Jesus died for you because He loves you.
- Jesus can save you from your sins.

Say

Can you think of a sin you've committed, something bad that you've done? You might think it is something that no one else knows about. You might even think you've gotten away with it, but God knows about it. The Bible tells us that everyone has sinned, and sin must be punished.

God gave His Son, Jesus, to take the punishment for your sin, including the one you're thinking about right now. The Bible says, "While we were still sinners, Christ died for us" (Rom. 5:8). Jesus died for you. He died on the cross to pay for your sins.

Jesus was willing to die for your sins because God loves you so much. The Bible says, "God so loved the world that he gave his one and only Son that whoever believes in him shall not perish but have eternal life" (John 3:16). To perish means to die. Jesus died for our sins so we do not have to. Jesus died for you because he loves you.

Jesus can save you from your sins. If we believe Jesus died for us, we can receive Him as our Savior. A savior is someone who saves your life when you can't save yourself. The Bible says, "Believe in the Lord Jesus, and you will be saved" (Acts 16:31). Jesus wants to save you because He loves you so much. Because He died for your sins, you can receive Him as your Savior.

Activity Options

Activity 1: *Jesus takes away sin.* Demonstrate again how sin leaves a permanent stain that we can't remove. Put several drops of food coloring in a large glass bowl of water. Explain how Jesus' death on the cross is the only way we can be rid of sin. Pour a small amount of bleach into the water and watch the coloring disappear. Talk about how Jesus can take away our sins if we ask Him into our lives. Optional: place the stained handkerchief from the previous lesson in the bleached water and watch it whiten.

Activity 2: *More words.* Review the symbols for "confess" and "repent." Add the two new symbols provided to show your students how to be saved. Show the children the picture of the cross. Talk about how we must believe Jesus died for our own sins. Show the children the symbol of a heart with the cross in it. Explain that when we ask Jesus to save us, He will come into our life and forgive us.

Action Point

Jesus died for your sins and wants to save you if you will believe in Him. Will you ask Jesus to forgive your sins?

Prayer

Dear Jesus, thank You for dying for us. We are sorry for our sins, and we believe in You. Help us to ask for Your forgiveness so that we might be saved. Thank You for saving us. Amen.

For Next Time

Jesus died for your sins, and He can forgive you. He will be your Savior, but He'll also be your friend. Do you think Jesus will be with you forever? We'll find out.

Salvation

Memory Verse
And surely I will be with you always, to the very end of the age.
Matthew 28:20

Jesus is my forever friend.

Before You Begin

■ Read John 15:12–15 and Revelation 3:20.
■ Review the Teaching Points to familiarize yourself with the ideas to emphasize in this session.
■ Read the session plan and select the elements that you will include.
■ Choose a Bible memorization technique from those listed in Section 1. Be sure to vary your teaching technique from session to session.
■ If you choose to include a learning activity, gather the materials you will need.
  • For Activity 1 you will need two pieces of paper, a marker, and music or a whistle (optional
  • For Activity 2 you will need copies of the friendship bracelet emblem, crayons, scissors, a hole punch, and yarn.

Teaching Points

■ You can invite Jesus into your life.
■ Jesus will be your friend forever.
■ You can be a friend to Jesus.

Say

Friends are special people. You enjoy being with a friend. You can tell a friend anything. We all need good friends. Jesus is our very special friend. If we ask Jesus to save us, He promises to come into our lives and to be with us forever. It's like inviting a friend over to stay. Jesus says, "I stand at the door and knock. If anyone hears my voice and opens the door, I will come in and eat with him, and he with me" (Rev. 3:20). Jesus wants to be your friend. You can invite Jesus into your life.

Jesus is the very best friend you can have. He will always be there to help you, and you can tell Jesus anything. Jesus will never leave you because He promises to stay. He says, "I will be with you always, to the very end of the age" (Matt. 28:20). Jesus will be your friend forever.

You can be a friend to Jesus too. If you never talked to your friends and never spent time with them, would they believe you were still their friend? No, you would never ignore your friends, so we should never ignore Jesus. We can talk to Him, and we should do what He says. Jesus said, "You are my friends if you do what I command" (John 15:14). It's good to know we have such a wonderful friend like Jesus and we can be His friends too. Jesus is our forever friend.

Activity Options

Activity 1: *Circle of Friends.* Write, "Jesus is my forever friend" on one sheet of paper. On a second sheet, write "Friends." Place the sheets opposite of each other on the floor. Have the children form a circle around the papers. Let the children move in the circle until you signal them to stop. The child standing in front of the paper that reads "Friends" may share something that they like to do with their friends. The child standing in front of the paper that reads, "Jesus is my forever friend" may share some way Jesus is a friend or a way to be a friend to Jesus.

Activity 2: Before class, prepare "Jesus is my Friend" bracelets for each child. On a piece of 1" x 4" paper print the words "Jesus is my Friend." Photo copy enough for each student to have one. Have each child cut out their "bracelet." Punch a hole in both ends and loop with yarn. Slip the "bracelet" onto each child's arm and tie the yarn. Tell the class that they can show their family and friends their "bracelets" and tell them about their Forever Friend, Jesus.

Action Point

Would you like to invite Jesus into your life so He can be your forever friend? If you ask Him to come in, He will.

Prayer

Dear Jesus, thank You for being our forever friend. Thank You that we can trust You to never leave us. Help us to be Your friend by taking time to talk to You and obeying what You command. Amen.

For Next Time

Jesus promises to never leave us; He is our forever friend. Did you know you could be a part of His family as well? We'll talk about that next time.

Salvation

34 I am part of God's family.

Before You Begin

- Read Luke 8:19–21, John 1:12–13, Romans 8:14–17, and 1 John 3:1–3.
- Review the Teaching Points to familiarize yourself with the ideas to emphasize in this session.
- Read the session plan and select the elements that you will include.
- Choose a Bible memorization technique from those listed in Section 1. Be sure to vary your teaching technique from session to session.
- If you choose to include a learning activity, gather the materials you will need.
  - For Activity 1 you will need brown and green construction paper, tape, scissors, glue, and a marker.
  - For Activity 2 you will need refreshments.

Teaching Points

- I am part of God's family.
- God wants you to be His child.
- Jesus makes it possible for you to join God's family.

Say

Isn't it wonderful to know that Jesus is your forever friend? But God has more good news for you. God wants you to be His child. When you believe in Jesus and ask Him to forgive your sins and come into your life, you become a part of God's family. The Bible says, "Everyone who believes that Jesus is the Christ is born of God" (1 John 5:1).

We use family trees to make a chart of what our families are like. In a family tree, your parents are the trunk of the tree, and you and all your brothers and sisters are the branches. God wants to add us to His family tree. Jesus says, "I am the vine; you are the branches" (John 15:5). Jesus makes it possible for you to join God's family. You are like a branch in His family tree.

God is our Heavenly Father and we are His children. That means everyone who believes in Jesus is our brother or sister. The Bible often calls believers "brothers" and "sisters," and just like all families, we can enjoy God's family. We can worship together, have meals together, and take care of each other. When talking about God's family, the Bible says they "ate together with glad and sincere hearts, praising God and enjoying the favor of all the people" (Acts 2:46–47). God has a big family, and if you believe in Jesus, you are a part of it.

Activity Options

Activity 1: *We are branches.* Use several sheets of brown construction paper taped together to cut a long winding shape to represent a vine. Cut enough shorter branches so there is one for each member of your class. Write "Jesus" on the vine and hang it in the classroom. Give each child a branch shape. Children may cut leaf shapes from green construction paper and glue them to their branch. Have the children write their names on their branches, and assist them in attaching them to the vine. Talk about how we are part of God's family tree.

Activity 2: *Fellowship.* Have a time of fellowship with your class. Serve refreshments, sing praises, pray, and practice calling each other "brother" and "sister." Talk about how God's family should enjoy each other's company.

Action Point

God wants you to be His child. Would you like to be a part of God's big family? Put your trust in Jesus.

Prayer

Dear God, thank You for being our Heavenly Father and for making a way for us to be Your children. Help us to put our trust in Jesus so we can be a part of Your family. Amen.

For Next Time

We are a part of God's family if we believe in Jesus. Did you know that God's family will all be together someday? Find out about it next week.

Salvation

Memory Verse

In my Father's house are many rooms; if it were not so, I would have told you. I am going there to prepare a place for you.
John 14:2

35 We can live with Jesus in heaven.

Before You Begin

■ Read Hebrews 11:13–16, 1 Peter 1:3–5, and Revelation 21–22:5.
■ Review the Teaching Points to familiarize yourself with the ideas to emphasize in this session.
■ Read the session plan and select the elements that you will include.
■ Choose a Bible memorization technique from those listed in Section 1. Be sure to vary your teaching technique from session to session.
■ If you choose to include a learning activity, gather the materials you will need.
  • For Activity 1 you will need drawing paper and crayons or markers.
  • For Activity 2 you will need several sheets of paper and a marker.

Teaching Points

■ We can live with Jesus in heaven.
■ Heaven is God's gift to believers.
■ Heaven is wonderful because God is there.

Say

Have you ever visited with a friend or family member that you haven't seen in a long time? You were probably excited to see them, and finally being with them made you very happy. How do you think you'd feel if you could visit with Jesus face to face? Someday you will be able to do that. You can live with Jesus in heaven. Jesus said that He was going to heaven to prepare a place for us (John 14:2). Jesus promises that He is making a place for you to live with Him.

Heaven will be a place for all God's children. If we put our trust in Jesus and we believe Him to save us from our sins so that we are His, then we have heaven as our inheritance. An inheritance is a gift given to you by your parents or grandparents. We do not earn it; we receive it as a gift. Jesus died and rose again so we could have an inheritance given by God our Father. We do not earn it; we receive it because we are His children. Heaven is God's gift to believers.

The Bible says heaven will be a place of joy. No one will be sad or crying. No bad thing can be there. Heaven is wonderful because God is there. The Bible says, "Now the dwelling of God is with men, and he will live with them. They will be his people, and God himself will be with them and be their God" (Rev. 21:3). In heaven, all of God's family will be together and we will live with Jesus.

Activity Options

Activity 1: *My room.* Give the children drawing paper and let them imagine what their room in heaven will look like. Discuss how Jesus himself is making their room. Let the children use crayons or markers to draw their imaginary room in heaven.

Activity 2: *In Heaven.* On several sheets of paper, write words that describe what we will experience in heaven, such as joy, peace, and living with Jesus. On others write words describing what we will not experience in heaven, such as crying, anger, sin, and loneliness. Mix the papers together. The children may take turns removing a paper from the stack and showing it to the class. Discuss what is written on the paper and whether or not it is something that will be in heaven. If the word describes heaven, have the child display the paper on the table or hang it on the wall. If the word does not describe heaven, have the child wad the paper up and throw it away. Continue until only the right descriptions are left.

Action Point

Heaven is God's gift to believers. Are you ready to live in heaven with Jesus someday? Believe in Jesus as your Savior.

Prayer

Dear God, thank You for making a place in heaven for us. Help each one of us to ask Jesus to forgive our sins so we can live with Him in heaven someday. Amen.

For Next Time

Someday, all of God's children will be together in heaven, but there is a place where God's children get together now. Find out where it is next time.

Church

36 People at church love God.

Before You Begin

- Read Acts 2:42–47 and 4:32–36.
- Review the Teaching Points to familiarize yourself with the ideas to emphasize in this session.
- Read the session plan and select the elements that you will include.
- Choose a Bible memorization technique from those listed in Section 1. Be sure to vary your teaching technique from session to session.
- If you choose to include a learning activity, prepare by reading the following instructions.
  - For Activity 1 make arrangements with an adult class to be interviewed by the children. Prompt the class on the concept.

Teaching Points

- People at church love God.
- People who love God can have church anywhere.
- People who love God also love church.

Say

If you like to do something, you probably want friends who enjoy doing the same thing you do. If you like to draw you would want to have friends who like to draw too. If you go to a ball game, don't you want to sit with others who cheer for the same team? People at church have something in common too. People at church love God.

People who love God can have church anywhere. After Jesus went back up into heaven, the people who believed in Him began to meet together. They didn't have a church building like we do today, but the Bible says, "All the believers were together" (Acts 2:44). The believers, or people who loved God, met in peoples' houses. In fact, some Christians still meet in houses. It doesn't matter where people meet. If the people love God, they can have church anywhere.

People who love God also love being in church. The Bible talks about early Christians. It says, "Every day they continued to meet together" (Acts 2:46). Can you imagine being in church every day? Those believers enjoyed being with each other because they all loved God. We can enjoy being at church too. We can enjoy being with others at church because people at church love God.

Activity Options

Activity 1: *Interviews.* Take your class to the adult classroom and have each child interview an adult student. Have the children ask the adults why they come to church. Children may also ask what their favorite part of church is. Return to your classroom and discuss what the adults said.

Activity 2: *In Heaven.* Teach your children this finger play. Help them follow the motions and respond to each phrase with, "They love God." You say, "Here is the church where the people meet." (Interlace fingers, putting palms together with fingers on the inside. Index fingers point up and touch at the tips to make a steeple.) Next say, "Open the doors of the church where the people meet." (Spread thumbs apart.) Lastly say, "Here are the people gathered inside." (Make the back of your hands touch so the interlaced fingers are sticking up.) Practice the finger play several times.

Action Point

People at church love God and love coming to church. Do you love coming to church because you love God?

Prayer

Dear God, thank You that we can meet together with others who love You. We're glad we can have church. Help us to always come because we love You. Amen.

For Next Time

People at church love God and gather together there, but what do they do? Find out next time.

Church

Memory Verse
Rejoice in the Lord always.
I will say it again: Rejoice!
Philippians 4:4

37 We worship God at church.

Before You Begin

- Read John 4:19–24 and Hebrews 10:19–25.
- Review the Teaching Points to familiarize yourself with the ideas to emphasize in this session.
- Read the session plan and select the elements that you will include.
- Choose a Bible memorization technique from those listed in Section 1. Be sure to vary your teaching technique from session to session.
- If you choose to include a learning activity, gather the materials you will need.
  - For Activity 2 you will need crepe paper streamers cut into twelve-inch lengths, tape, and pencils or short dowel rods.

Teaching Points

- We worship God at church.
- We worship by celebrating that Jesus is our Savior.
- It is good that we worship together.

Say

When we come to church, we take part in a lot of activities. We sing and read from God's Word, the Bible. We pray and take an offering. Then the pastor stands and talks about God. Do you ever wonder what it is all for? We come to church because we love God. When we are at church, we worship God.

When we worship God, that means we think more of Him than anyone or anything else. Jesus said, "Worship the Lord your God and serve him only" (Luke 4:8). God is the only one we should worship. We honor Him because He is our Heavenly Father. When we worship, we also celebrate what Jesus has done for us. The Bible says, "Rejoice in the Lord always" (Phil. 4:4). We worship by celebrating that Jesus is our Savior.

It is good that we worship together. You can worship God when you are by yourself, but when we worship God together at church, we encourage each other to love God more. The Bible says, "Let us not give up meeting together . . . but let us encourage one another" (Heb. 10:25). We should never stop coming to church. We worship God at church. It is good to worship God and celebrate with others what Jesus has done for us.

Activity Options

Activity 1: *Reverence.* Take your class on a walking tour of the church sanctuary. Look at the hymnals, go up on the platform, and let the children stand at the podium or kneel at the altar. Talk about how people worship God in the sanctuary. One way we can worship God is to show respect for the church where we worship Him. Discuss ways to show reverence to God. Examples include not running in the sanctuary, climbing on the altar, or scribbling in the hymnals.

Activity 2: *Celebrate.* Give each child about a half dozen crepe paper streamers, cut about 12 inches in length. Twist the ends of the streamers together and tape them to a pencil or short dowel rod to form a pompom. Talk about how we can worship by celebrating that Jesus is our Savior. Let the children make up simple cheers and shake their pompoms to praise and worship Jesus.

Action Point

We worship God at church. Can you think of ways that you and your friends can worship God and celebrate Jesus?

Prayer

Dear God, we want to worship You. Help us to celebrate all Your goodness to us and to rejoice with others that Jesus is our Savior. Help us to always show respect for Your house. Amen.

For Next Time

We worship God at church, but how can we celebrate what Jesus did for us if we don't know about it? Where can we learn about Him? Let's talk about it next time.

Church

Memory Verse
Day after day . . .
they never stopped teaching
. . . the good news that
Jesus is the Christ.
Acts 5:42

38 We learn about Jesus at church.

Before You Begin

- Read Acts 5:17–42 and Romans 10:14–15.
- Review the Teaching Points to familiarize yourself with the ideas to emphasize in this session.
- Read the session plan and select the elements that you will include.
- Choose a Bible memorization technique from those listed in Section 1. Be sure to vary your teaching technique from session to session.
- If you choose to include a learning activity, gather the materials you will need.
  - For Activity 1 you will need paper bags, a Bible, a Sunday school workbook or different pictures depicting events in Jesus' life, and several objects, such as a baseball, textbook, or video game.
  - For Activity 2 you will need paper and crayons.

Teaching Points

- We can learn about Jesus in church.
- The church spreads the good news about Jesus.
- There is always more to learn about Jesus.

Say

How did you first learn about Jesus? Did your mom and dad tell you about Him? Did someone read to you from the Bible? It is good for everyone to learn about Jesus, and we can learn about Jesus in church.

We all need to learn about Jesus so we can come to know Him as our Savior. The church is made up of people who love Jesus. Jesus wants the church to tell everyone how He died to save them. This message that Jesus died for our sins is called the good news. The church spreads the good news. It teaches about Jesus so people can know Him. People can't get to know Jesus if they've never heard of Him. The Bible asks, "How can they hear without someone preaching to them?" (Rom. 10:14). It is good for everyone to hear the good news so they can know Jesus as their Savior.

The church will never stop teaching about Jesus. There is always more that we can learn about Him. The Christians in the Bible always talked about Jesus. The Bible says, "Day after day...they never stopped teaching...the good news that Jesus is the Christ" (Acts 5:42).

Jesus wants us to know Him. To know Him, we need to learn about Him, and we can learn about Jesus at church.

Activity Options

Activity 1: *What we learn.* Before class begins, place objects, such as a baseball, textbook, or video game in paper bags. Place objects, such as a Bible, pictures depicting events in Jesus' life, or a Sunday school workbook in other bags. Fold the tops of the bags down and sit them together. Have the children take turns choosing a bag and discovering what is inside. Talk about each item and whether or not it is something we can learn about in church.

Activity 2: Give each child a plain piece of paper, pencil and crayons and have them draw a picture of their church. If they have trouble thinking of what to draw—ask them questions: What are some things you do at your church? Who are the people you see at your church? What does our church look like? What do you like most about your church? After they have drawn their churches, ask them if Jesus is at their church? Have them draw Jesus somewhere in their picture of their church.

Action Point

We learn about Jesus in church. What things have you learned about Jesus? Have you asked Him to be your Savior?

Prayer

Dear God, thank You for giving us a church so we can learn about Jesus. Help us to learn about Him so we can know Him as our Savior. Amen.

For Next Time

When we learn about Jesus in church, we can worship Him and celebrate what He did for us. Would you like to know some ways to worship Him? We'll learn next time.

Church

Memory Verse
Enter his gates with
thanksgiving and his
courts with praise.
Psalm 100:4

39 We worship God by singing and praying.

Before You Begin

- Read Psalm 100:1–5, Ephesians 5:19–21, Colossians 3:15–17, and 1 Thessalonians 5:16–18.
- Review the Teaching Points to familiarize yourself with the ideas to emphasize in this session.
- Read the session plan and select the elements that you will include.
- Choose a Bible memorization technique from those listed in Section 1. Be sure to vary your teaching technique from session to session.
- If you choose to include a learning activity, gather the materials you will need.
  - For Activity 1 you will need plastic eggs that open, small plastic beads, tape, and worship chorus music and a music player (optional).
  - For Activity 2 you will need a small potted tree, a small artificial Christmas tree, or a branch in a pot braced by stones to make a "tree." You will also need paper, crayons, and ribbon.

Teaching Points

- We can worship God by singing.
- We can worship God by praying.
- We can sing and pray together.

Say

Did you know that God likes to hear you sing? You may not think you are a very good singer, or maybe you think you don't know many songs. It doesn't matter. We can worship God by singing. The Bible says, "sing and make music in your heart to the Lord" (Eph. 5:19). Singing is also a good way to show our joy. The Bible says, "shout for joy to the Lord" (Ps. 100:1). God is pleased when we worship Him with songs.

God also likes to hear you pray. God wants you to tell Him what you need. You can also ask God for help. But God also likes to hear you say thank you for all that He has done. We can worship God by praying. The Bible says, "give thanks to him and praise his name" (Ps. 100:4). God is pleased when we offer prayers of thanksgiving.

You can certainly sing by yourself and pray when you are alone. But God also likes to hear His children sing and pray together. Have you ever gotten excited or happy because someone else was? The Bible says "speak to one another with psalms, hymns and spiritual songs" (Eph. 5:19). We can sing and pray together. When we do, we are helping others sing and pray too. God is pleased when we worship Him by singing and praying.

Activity Options

Activity 1: *Simple shakers.* Make simple shakers by giving each child a plastic egg and a handful of plastic beads. Put the beads in one end of the egg and put the two egg halves together. Secure the egg with tape. Use shakers as rhythm instruments as you make a joyful noise, singing choruses together.

Activity 2: *Thank you tree.* Obtain a small potted tree, a small artificial Christmas tree, or place a branch in a pot and brace it with stones to create a tree. Explain that this will be a "thank you" tree. Give each child a small piece of paper and crayons. Have them make a drawing of something they are thankful for. Children may share what they are thankful for, then roll the sheet up, tie a ribbon around it, and hang the paper on the tree. Continue until the tree is full. Finish with prayer, thanking God for all the things represented on the tree. Keep the tree in your classroom and continue to add to it.

Action Point

God is pleased when we worship Him by singing and praying. What things has He done for you that you can praise Him for?

Prayer

Dear God, thank You for all You've done for us. Help us to always offer You prayers of thanksgiving and remember to sing for joy as we worship You. Amen.

For Next Time

Singing and praying are two ways to worship God. Can you think of another way we can worship God? We'll find out what it is next time.

Church

Memory Verse
Let the word of Christ
dwell in you richly.
Colossians 3:16

40 We worship God by learning His Word.

Before You Begin

■ Read 2 Timothy 2:14–15 and Colossians 3:16.
■ Review the Teaching Points to familiarize yourself with the ideas to emphasize in this session.
■ Read the session plan and select the elements that you will include.
■ Choose a Bible memorization technique from those listed in Section 1. Be sure to vary your teaching technique from session to session.
■ If you choose to include a learning activity, gather the materials you will need.
  • For Activity 1 you will need manila folders, a marker, crayons, stickers, a stapler, and index cards.
  • For Activity 2 make arrangements with your pastor to meet with your class in the pastor's study.

Teaching Points

■ We learn God's Word because we love God.
■ We worship God by learning His Word.
■ God gives us people to help teach His Word.

Say

Have you ever received a letter from someone you love? Maybe your grandparents mailed you a birthday card, and you could hardly wait to open it. We can be excited about God's Word too because when we open it we learn all the good things He has promised us. We learn God's Word because we love God.

When we love God, He is more important to us than anyone else in the world. That is why we worship Him. We worship God by learning His Word. The Bible says, "Let the word of Christ dwell in you richly" (Col. 3:16). Richly is a word that means there is a lot. God wants us to know a lot of the Bible. He is pleased when we learn His Word.

God gives people to help teach us His word. We study the Bible in at church. We listen to the pastor preach from the Bible during the service. The Bible says Jesus gave "some to be pastors and teachers to prepare God's people for works of service" (Eph. 4:11–12). When we know God's Word we can serve Him better.

We learn God's Word at church from people who help teach us. We learn God's Word because we love Him and want to worship Him.

Activity Options

Activity 1: *Word pockets*. Give each child a manila folder with the words, "I learn God's Word" written on the front. Children may decorate the folders with crayons and stickers. Staple the edges of the folder, leaving the top open so it forms a "pocket." Ask each child to think of truths they've already learned from God's Word. Write each child's responses on index cards and give them to the child to place in their pocket. Give each child a few blank cards so they can continue to fill their pockets with things they learn from God's Word.

Activity 2: *Pastor visit*. Take your class to meet with the pastor in his or her study. Have the pastor talk about how God called him or her to preach so that people can learn God's Word. The pastor may show the children how ministers study to share God's Word correctly.

Action Point

God gives people to help us learn the Bible so we can worship Him. Do you love Him enough to learn it?

Prayer

Dear God, thank You for pastors and teachers who help us learn Your word. Help us to study so that Your Word will dwell in us richly and we can worship You. Amen.

For Next Time

When we learn God's Word, we are able to serve Him better. Can you think of some ways you can serve Him by helping others at church? Find out what you can do next time.

Church

Memory Verse
Therefore encourage
one another and build
each other up.
1 Thessalonians 5:11

41 We help others at church.

Before You Begin

- Read 1 Thessalonians 5:11–14, 1Timothy 4:12, and Hebrews 10:24–25.
- Review the Teaching Points to familiarize yourself with the ideas to emphasize in this session.
- Read the session plan and select the elements that you will include.
- Choose a Bible memorization technique from those listed in Section 1. Be sure to vary your teaching technique from session to session.
- If you choose to include a learning activity, gather the materials you will need.
  - For Activity 2 you will need name tag stickers.

Teaching Points

- We can help others at church.
- We can be an example to others.
- We can encourage others.

Say

The church is God's family. Just like any family, there are grownups and children, young and old. There are people of all ages, but everyone is important and everyone helps out. Do you know you can be a helper in God's family? You may wonder how you can help others when you are a child, but your age doesn't matter. Young or old, we can help others at church.

You can be an example to others at church. An example is a pattern for others to follow. When others see how you believe in Jesus, how you try to please God, and how you worship Him at church, it will help them to believe in Jesus. They will want to worship too. The Bible says, "Don't let anyone look down on you because you are young, but set an example for the believers" (1 Tim. 4:12). You can be an example even though you are young.

You can encourage others at church. That means you can help them to feel happy and have hope. You can offer a friendly smile and shake someone's hand. You can hold doors open for older people or walk with them to their seat. You could even talk to someone who is sitting alone. The Bible says, "encourage one another and build each other up" (1 Thess. 5:11).

You are not too young to help others at church. You can be an example to others and encourage others to follow Jesus.

Activity Options

Activity 1: *Greeters.* Enlist your class to help greet people who are entering the church for services. Let the children welcome people, shake their hands, and pass out church bulletins.

Activity 2: *Class helpers.* Assign each of your students a job to do so they can help out in class. Before class begins, write each child's job on a name tag sticker. Give the children their sticker to wear, and explain their job as they arrive for class. Let the children help in class with jobs, such as handing out papers or crayons, sharpening pencils, picking up trash, erasing the board, or anything appropriate for your classroom. During activity time, ask your students how it felt to be a helper. Did they feel important? Did it help them to feel like a part of the class? Be sure to also tell your children how much you appreciated their help.

Action Point

We help others at church. Will you be an example to others in worship, and will you encourage someone today?

Prayer

Dear God, thank You for giving us a church family. Help us to be an example by helping others and encouraging them to believe in You. Amen.

For Next Time

You can help others at church, but people need God's help everyday. Do you want to know how you can help others get God's help? Find out next time.

The Christian Life

Memory Verse
Dear brothers and
sisters, pray for us.
1 Thessalonians 5:25, NLT

I can pray for others.

Before You Begin

■ Read John 17:20–23, Ephesians 6:18–20, and James 5:14–16.
■ Review the Teaching Points to familiarize yourself with the ideas to emphasize in this session.
■ Read the session plan and select the elements that you will include.
■ Choose a Bible memorization technique from those listed in Section 1. Be sure to vary your teaching technique from session to session.
■ If you choose to include a learning activity, gather the materials you will need.
  • For Activity 1 you will need paper and markers.
  • For Activity 2 you will need blank greeting cards with envelopes, and crayons or pencils.

Teaching Points

■ Jesus prayed for others.
■ You can pray for others' needs.
■ You put others first when you pray for them.

Say

God wants us to pray, and He hears us when we talk to Him. When you pray, you can thank God for all He's done. You can tell God the things you need. You can also pray for others. Jesus prayed for others, and He is our example. He said, "I pray also for those who will believe in me" (John 17:20). He prayed for people to believe in Him so they could be saved. If Jesus thought it was important to pray for others, we should too.

You can pray for people's needs. If someone is sick, you can pray for God to make them well. If someone needs to ask Jesus to forgive them, you can pray that Jesus would help them make that decision. You can pray for people who ask you to pray for them, and you can pray for people you don't know. The Bible says, "The earnest prayer of a righteous person has great power and wonderful results" (James 5:16, NLT). God will hear you pray for others.

When you pray for someone, your prayer may not always be answered the way you think it should be. That is all right because God knows what is best for the person you are praying for. What matters is that you pray for them. You put others first when you pray for them. When you pray for others, it shows that you care for them. God is pleased when we pray for others.

Activity Options

Activity 1: *Prayer list.* Write, "I can pray for others" at the top of a sheet of paper. Help your class make a prayer list of people they can pray for. You can make suggestions, such as praying for parents, brothers and sisters, and the pastor. Write down any specific requests any child may have. Make a copy of the completed list for each of your students. Encourage the children to pray for the people on the list every day. Finish by praying for the people on the list in class.

Activity 2: *Prayer cards.* Explain that people can be encouraged if they know we are praying for them. Help each child think of someone they can pray for, and have a prayer time in class. Give the children blank greeting cards, and help them write the words, "I prayed for you today" inside. Put the cards in envelopes, and write the person's name on the outside. Let the children give their cards to the person they prayed for.

Action Point

God is pleased when we pray for others. Who can you pray for this week? Remember to pray for them every day.

Prayer

Dear God, thank You that You hear and answer our prayers. Help us to follow Jesus' example and put others first by praying for them. Amen.

For Next Time

Praying for others is a good way to show you care for them. You can show you care for the church through giving. Find out how next time.

The Christian Life

Memory Verse
God loves a cheerful giver.
2 Corinthians 9:7

43 I can bring an offering to church.

Before You Begin

- Read Mark 12:11–44, Luke 6:38, and 2 Corinthians 8:1–12.
- Review the Teaching Points to familiarize yourself with the ideas to emphasize in this session.
- Read the session plan and select the elements that you will include.
- Choose a Bible memorization technique from those listed in Section 1. Be sure to vary your teaching technique from session to session.
- If you choose to include a learning activity, gather the materials you will need.
  - For Activity 1 you will need small boxes with lids or small coffee tins with lids, paper, tape, and markers or crayons.

Teaching Points

- People bring offerings because they love God.
- People give offerings willingly.
- Peoples' offerings bless others.

Say

Have you ever wondered why we pass an offering plate at church? Why do you think people put money in the plate? The offering plate is passed around so people can have a chance to give an offering to God. An offering is a gift, usually money, which people give to God. The church uses the offerings to do God's work. People bring offerings because they love God. They also love the church. You can bring an offering to church too.

You wouldn't force someone to give you a gift. If you did that, it wouldn't be a gift would it? God doesn't force us to bring offerings. We give our offerings willingly. The Bible says, "God loves a cheerful giver" (2 Cor. 9:7). Some people are able to give a lot for an offering. Others can only give a little. No matter what you bring to God for an offering, He wants you to be happy about giving it.

Your offerings bless others. You may never see what your offering is used for, but God knows. God will also bless you for being a giver. The Bible says, "Give, and it will be given to you" (Luke 6:38). That doesn't mean God will give you money. But as you give to help others in need, God will make sure you have everything you need too.

You can be a cheerful giver. You can bring an offering to church and God will bless you for it.

Activity Options

Activity 1: *Offering box.* Ahead of time, prepare a small box with a lid by cutting a slit in the lid so coins will fit through it (a small coffee tin with a plastic lid also works well). Give one to each child. Wrap paper around the box and secure with tape. Help the children to write "My Offering" on the box. Decorate the boxes as you wish. Children may take the boxes home to save money for offerings.

Activity 2: *Earn an offering.* Explain to the children that they can earn money for an offering. Have each child think of something they can do around the house to earn money. Ideas include sweeping, dusting, or helping to put away clothes. Each child acts out the chore they are thinking of while the others try to guess what the action is. Encourage the children to do something at home to earn money for an offering. You may also want to contact the parents of each child so they can cooperate in helping the child earn money for an offering.

Action Point

You can bring an offering to church. What can you do this week to earn an offering you can give to God?

Prayer

Dear God, thank You for giving us everything we need. We want to bring our offerings to church as a gift to You because we love You. Help us to be cheerful givers. Amen.

For Next Time

We can bring offerings to church because we love God. We can bring a friend to church because God loves them. Find out more next time.

The Christian Life

44 God helps me do what is right.

Before You Begin

■ Read Matthew 28:19, John 1:40–46, and John 4:1–42.
■ Review the Teaching Points to familiarize yourself with the ideas to emphasize in this session.
■ Read the session plan and select the elements that you will include.
■ Choose a Bible memorization technique from those listed in Section 1. Be sure to vary your teaching technique from session to session.
■ If you choose to include a learning activity, gather the materials you will need.
   • For Activity 1 you will need an invitation postcard for each child.

Teaching Points

■ We can invite a friend to church.
■ Your friend can meet Jesus at church.
■ Jesus wants us to invite others.

Say

Have you ever had special news that you couldn't wait to tell someone else about? Have you ever gotten a gift that you couldn't wait to share with a friend? At church we hear the good news that Jesus loves us. We learn about the gift of salvation. We can share this good news with others because Jesus' gift is for everyone. We can invite a friend to church.

Your friends can meet Jesus at church. In the Bible, a man named Philip met Jesus. He was so excited that he told his friend Nathanael to "come and see" (John 1:46). He wanted Nathanael to meet Jesus too. When your friends know Jesus, they will be glad you invited them to church. In the Bible, a man named David said, "I rejoiced with those who said to me, 'Let us go to the house of the Lord' (Ps. 122:1). You can rejoice with your friends too.

Jesus wants us to invite others. He told His followers, "Go into all the world and preach the good news" (Mark 16:15–16). You may not be able to go to other parts of the world because you are young. But you can go to a friend. You may never be a preacher, but you can invite a friend to church to hear the good news.

Activity Options

Activity 1: *Invitations.* Give each child an invitation postcard. Read what the invitations say, and have the children think of a friend they can invite to church. Help the children write their friend's name on the invitation. Encourage the children to give or mail the postcard to their friend and invite them to church and Sunday school.

Activity 2: *Friends Day.* Ahead of time, make up a short letter to send to parents explaining this idea. Plan a "Friends Day" with your class. Let the children help decorate the room and move in extra chairs for the friends who will be there next week. Let the children choose a special song or activity to do with their friends and help plan what kind of refreshments to serve. Have the children role play with each other to practice inviting someone to church. Pass out the letters to the children to give to their parents.

Action Point

Jesus wants to meet all your friends. Can you think of someone to invite to church? Invite them to church this week.

Prayer

Dear God, thank You that we can learn to know You at church. Help us to invite our friends to church so they can know You and worship with us. Amen.

For Next Time

It is right that we invite our friends to church. We can always do what is right if we let God help us. We'll talk about that next time.

The Christian Life

Memory Verse
The Lord is with me;
he is my helper.
Psalm 118:7

45 God helps me do what is right.

Before You Begin

■ Read 1 Corinthians 10:13, Hebrews 2:18, and Hebrews 4:14–16.
■ Review the Teaching Points to familiarize yourself with the ideas to emphasize in this session.
■ Read the session plan and select the elements that you will include.
■ Choose a Bible memorization technique from those listed in Section 1. Be sure to vary your teaching technique from session to session.
■ If you choose to include a learning activity, gather the materials you will need.
  • For Activity 2 you will need paper lunch sacks and a small reward.

Teaching Points

■ God helps me do what is right.
■ God helps me do right when tempted to do wrong.
■ I can do right even when it's hard.

Say

God is pleased when we obey Him. He wants us to do what is right. Doing what is right may be what you want to do, but it's not always easy. You need help. The Bible says "the Lord is with me; he is my helper" (Ps. 118:7). God helps you do what is right. When you do what is right, you please God.

Sometimes you will be tempted to do wrong. When you are tempted, you think very strongly about doing something that is wrong. You must choose to do what is right. Jesus was tempted just like we are, but He always chose to do what was right. Jesus understands how it feels to be tempted to do wrong. The Bible says that because Jesus was tempted "he is able to help those who are being tempted" (Heb. 2:18). You can ask God to help you choose to do right like Jesus did. God helps you do right when tempted to do wrong.

Sometimes it is hard to do what is right. Pretend you broke a window. Would it be hard to tell your parents? Would it be right to pretend you didn't do it? You must always do what is right, even if it is hard. God wants to help you. The Bible says we can come to God "and find grace to help us in our time of need" (Heb. 4:16). God helps you do right even when it's hard. You can do what is right.

Activity Options

Activity 1: *Reminder rhyme.* Teach your class the following motion rhyme to help them remember they have God's help to do what's right. Say,

> If you're marching with the pack (march in place)
> And you don't know how to act (shrug shoulders)
> Then stop!" (hold up hand, palm facing out)
> Think about it (point to head)
> God will keep you on His track! (point up, smile, and nod head)

Activity 2: *God helps.* Choose one student to be the helper and one student to wait outside the classroom. Give the class paper lunch sacks. Put a reward in one of the lunch sacks. Have the other student enter the room. The children with the sacks must try to trick that child into thinking their sack has the reward. The student points to any sack and asks the helper to tell him yes or no. He should not take a sack unless he is sure it is the right one. Talk about how God can help us do what is right no matter what.

Action Point

God will help you choose to do what is right. Why not ask Him for His help today?

Prayer

Dear God, thank You for being our helper. Help us to do what is right though we are tempted to do wrong. Help us to do what is right when it is hard. We want to please You. Amen.

For Next Time

God helps us do what is right. One right thing we can do is to help others. Find out about it next time.

The Christian Life

Memory Verse
As we have opportunity,
let us do good to
all people.
Galatians 6:10

46 I can help others.

Before You Begin

- Read Matthew 25:34–40, Luke 6:27–36, James 2:14–17, and 1 Peter 4:9–10.
- Review the Teaching Points to familiarize yourself with the ideas to emphasize in this session.
- Read the session plan and select the elements that you will include.
- Choose a Bible memorization technique from those listed in Section 1. Be sure to vary your teaching technique from session to session.
- If you choose to include a learning activity, gather the materials you will need.
  - For Activity 1 you will need a poster board, a drinking glass for tracing circles, scissors, one-inch ribbon cut in strips, markers or crayons, and two-sided tape.
  - For Activity 2 you will need a large box, plain paper to wrap the box, and markers or crayons.

Teaching Points

- I can help others.
- Helping others shows my faith in God.
- Whatever I do for others, I do for Jesus.

Say

Isn't it good to know we have people around who can help us when we need it? Who helps you when you need help? Does your mom or your dad help you? Do people at church help you? God is pleased when we help each other. The Bible says, "As we have opportunity, let us do good to all people" (Gal. 6:10). That means we should help each other whenever we have the chance. Everyone needs help sometime. You can help others.

When you help others, you show that you care about them. They will also see how you believe and trust in God. When you believe and trust

God, it is called faith. The Bible says, "I will show you my faith by what I do" (James 2:18). Helping others shows your faith in God. It will help others believe in Him too.

If Jesus needed help, wouldn't you help Him? If He were hungry, wouldn't you give Him something to eat? If He were lonely, wouldn't you visit Him? Did you know that when you help others, it's just as if you're helping Jesus? Jesus said, "When you did it to one of the least of these my brothers and sisters, you were doing it to me" (Matt. 25:40, NLT). Whatever you do for others, you do for Jesus.

When you help others, you please God and show your faith. You can help others.

Activity Options

Activity 1: *Helper badges.* Trace around a drinking glass to make circles on poster board. Cut out a circle for each student. Help the students write, "I can help" on the circle. Glue a strip of one-inch wide ribbon to the back of the circle, letting it hang down below the circle. Use two-sided tape to stick the badges to the children's clothing. Children can wear their badges to show they are helpers. Let the children think of ways they can help, and encourage them to offer their help to friends and family.

Activity 2: *Help someone.* Prepare a box in your classroom to gather food, clothing, or items to be given to a local food pantry, thrift store, or mission. Wrap the box in paper and write on it, "I can help others." Let each child write his or her name on the box. Encourage the children to bring in the items you've decided to collect, and send a note home to parents explaining the project. Talk about how their actions will help others.

Action Point

We please God and show others our faith when we help people. What can you do to help others?

Prayer

Dear God, thank You for giving us a chance to help others. When we help others, let us always remember that what we do for them, we are doing for You. Amen.

For Next Time

The more you show your faith in God by helping others, the more you become like Jesus. Did you know you could grow to be like Him? We'll talk about that next time.

The Christian Life

47 I can grow like Jesus.

Before You Begin

- Read Matthew 11:28–30, 1 Corinthians 11:1, and Hebrews 12:1–3.
- Review the Teaching Points to familiarize yourself with the ideas to emphasize in this session.
- Read the session plan and select the elements that you will include.
- Choose a Bible memorization technique from those listed in Section 1. Be sure to vary your teaching technique from session to session.
- If you choose to include a learning activity, gather the materials you will need.
  - For Activity 2 you will need a dry sponge, a bowl or a towel, and a cup of water.

Teaching Points

- You can grow like Jesus.
- Jesus is our example.
- We grow like Jesus by faith.

Say

We've talked about how Jesus didn't stay a little baby. He grew up. Your body is growing too, and one day you will be grown up. But there is another way you can grow. You can grow like Jesus. Jesus wants you to grow like Him now, and He also wants you to keep growing like Him even when you are grown up. You can never finish growing like Jesus.

Jesus himself teaches us how to grow like Him. He is our example. Remember that an example is a pattern for others to follow. In the Bible, a man named Paul taught others about Jesus. He said, "follow my example, as I follow the example of Christ" (1 Cor. 11:1). We can see Jesus' example when we learn about Him in the Bible. You can follow Jesus' example by obeying all His teachings and treating others the way Jesus did. When you do, you're growing like Him.

The Bible says, "Let us fix our eyes on Jesus, the author and perfecter of our faith" (Heb. 12:2). Remember that faith is our belief and trust in God. Jesus is the author of our faith. That means Jesus helps us believe. Jesus is the perfecter of our faith. That means He helps us trust God completely. We grow like Jesus by faith. We follow Him because we have faith, and the more we follow Jesus, the more faith He gives us. You can grow like Jesus.

Activity Options

Activity 1: *Follow an example.* Choose one child to be the leader. The other children should go anywhere the leader goes and copy any motions the leader makes. Talk about how the followers had to keep their eyes on the leader so they would know what to do and just how to do it. Compare this with how we must keep our eyes on Jesus so we can grow like Him.

Activity 2: *Faith Grows.* Show the children a dry sponge. Talk about how our faith may start out small, but it can grow as we follow Jesus. Let the children think of ways they can grow like Jesus. Examples include treating people with kindness, obeying Jesus' word, and learning about Him. Each time the children suggest a way, pour a little water on the sponge and watch it expand. (Place the sponge in a bowl or on a towel to catch any extra water.) Use this to demonstrate how our faith grows a little more each time we follow Jesus' example.

Action Point

Jesus is our example. Will you carefully do what Jesus would do? If so, you'll have more faith and you'll grow like Jesus.

Prayer

Dear Jesus, thank You for being our example so we can grow like You. Help us to follow You so that we will have more faith. Help us to keep growing like You all our lives. Amen.

For Next Time

You can grow like Jesus so that you'll be able to treat others like He would. Growing like Jesus will help you love your family. We'll talk about that next time.

The Christian Life

Memory Verse
Let us not love with words or tongue but with actions and in truth.
1 John 3:18

48   I can love my family.

Before You Begin

- Read Exodus 20:12, 1 Corinthians 13:1–8, 1 Timothy 5:3–8, and 1 John 3:11–24.
- Review the Teaching Points to familiarize yourself with the ideas to emphasize in this session.
- Read the session plan and select the elements that you will include.
- Choose a Bible memorization technique from those listed in Section 1. Be sure to vary your teaching technique from session to session.
- If you choose to include a learning activity, gather the materials you will need.
  - For Activity 1 you will need drawing paper and crayons.
  - For Activity 2 you will need blank note cards, crayons, and stickers.

Teaching Points

- I can love my family.
- My family is special to me.
- I can show my family love by treating them kindly.
- God tells me how to love.

Say

We've learned that God made each of our families different. Families are special. You may have many friends all your life, but you have only one family. You will always be a part of your family. Your family is special to you.

God wants us to love our families. Saying we love our family is not enough. We show we love them by how we treat them. The Bible says, "Let us not love with words or tongue but with actions and in truth" (1 John 3:18). If you say you love your family but you treat them badly, what does that show? You show your family love by treating them kindly.

God tells us how to love in the Bible. When we love, we are patient. That means we don't always have to be first. We are kind. When we love, we don't brag about ourselves or get angry when someone has something we want. When we love, we are not rude or selfish, and we don't stay mad at each other. When we love, we want to make sure our families have everything they need. The Bible says, "Love never fails" (1 Cor. 13:8). You don't have to worry about treating your family wrong if you love them. The more you love your family members, the more special they'll be to you. You can love your family.

Activity Options

Activity 1: *Family portraits.* Give each child paper and crayons and let them draw their family. Let the children compare their pictures and talk about how their family is special to them. Discuss with the children ways they can show love to their family members.

Activity 2: *Love notes.* Give each child a blank note card to make a love note for each member of his or her family. Use crayons, heart stickers, or anything else to make the notes look special. Help the children write each family member's name on the note. Encourage the children to give their love notes to their family members and say something kind or give a hug when they deliver them.

Action Point

You can love your family. What ways can you think of to show your family you love them this week?

Prayer

Dear God, thank You for our families. Help us to not only say we love our families but to also show that we love them as well. Thank You for telling us how to love in the Bible. Amen.

For Next Time

You can love your family, but sometimes, just like doing what is right, you need help. God will help you with anything; all you need to do is ask. Find out about that next time.

The Christian Life

Memory Verse
The Lord is near to
all who call on him.
Psalm 145:18

49   I can ask God for help.

Before You Begin

■ Read Psalm 121:1–8, Isaiah 41:10, 13, and 1 Peter 5:7.
■ Review the Teaching Points to familiarize yourself with the ideas to emphasize in this session.
■ Read the session plan and select the elements that you will include.
■ Choose a Bible memorization technique from those listed in Section 1. Be sure to vary your teaching technique from session to session.
■ If you choose to include a learning activity, gather the materials you will need.
  • For Activity 1 you will need one small rock.
  • For Activity 2 you will need a small stone for each child, and a container with lid.

Teaching Points

■ I can ask God for help.
■ I can give my fears to God.
■ God tells me how to love.

Say

It's good to have someone to help us when we need it. But sometimes you may think you have a problem no one can help you with. It may be that you don't know how to fix the problem, or maybe it is something you are just worried about. There is someone you can turn to, someone you can always ask to help you. That someone is God. You can ask God for help.

God cares about your problems. The Bible says, "Cast all your anxiety on him because he cares for you" (1 Pet. 5:7). To cast means to throw something away from you. Anxiety is another word for your worries or fears. You can throw your fears on God. When we give God our problems, we don't have to worry about them anymore.

God wants to help with our problems, and He waits for us to ask Him for help. The Bible says, "The Lord is near to all who call on him" (Ps. 145:18). Sometimes God helps by fixing the problem. Sometimes He helps us by being with us while we suffer through our troubles. The Bible says, "God is our refuge and strength, an ever-present help in trouble" (Ps. 46:1). He will be with us while we are going through a difficult time. When you have a problem, you can remember God is near, just waiting to help you. You can ask God for help.

Activity Options

Activity 1: *Give it to God.* Show the children a small rock that will fit in your hand. Explain that you are worried you might lose the rock or crack it. Ask the children to help you keep the rock safe. Pretend to give it to them, always pulling your hand back. Hold the rock tightly in your hand. Use this object lesson to demonstrate how we can't hold on to our problems, but we've got to give them to God

Activity 2: *Cast your cares.* Give each child a small stone. Have the children think of something for which they would like to ask God's help. It can be a problem, something they are worried about, or something that makes them afraid. Have a time of silent prayer and encourage the children to give the situation to God. If possible, have the children throw or cast their stones away outside. Or have a container with a lid ready, and let the children toss their stones into the container and seal it.

Action Point

You can ask God for help. What are you holding onto that God can help you with? Why not give it to Him?

Prayer

Dear God, thank You that You are ready and waiting to help us with our problems. Help us to cast all our fears on You, knowing You are able to help us. Amen.

For Next Time

Sometimes people don't ask for God's help because they don't know He can help them. That's why it's important to tell others about Jesus. We'll learn more next week.

The Christian Life

Memory Verse
Come and listen, all you who fear God; let me tell you what he has done for me.
Psalm 66:16

50 I can tell my friends about Jesus.

Before You Begin

- Read Psalm 51:10–13, Matthew 28:16–20, and Acts 1:8.
- Review the Teaching Points to familiarize yourself with the ideas to emphasize in this session.
- Read the session plan and select the elements that you will include.
- Choose a Bible memorization technique from those listed in Section 1. Be sure to vary your teaching technique from session to session.
- If you choose to include a learning activity, gather the materials you will need.
  - For Activity 1 you will need one thin leather strip for each child (as for stringing jewelry) and six pony beads for each child in the following colors: black, red, white, green, and two yellow.

Teaching Points

- You can tell your friends about Jesus.
- Tell your friends what Jesus has done for you.
- You can tell your friends how to be saved.

Say

Jesus wants everyone to know how He died to save them from their sins. He has given His followers the important job of telling others this good news. Before He went back to heaven, Jesus told his disciples, "You will be my witnesses" (Acts 1:8). Witnesses tell what they know and what has happened to them. If you are a follower of Jesus, you can share in this important job. You can be a witness. You can tell your friends about Jesus.

When you talk about Jesus, do you wonder what you should say? Telling your friends about Jesus is easy. Has He forgiven your sins? How does He help you everyday? These are things you can talk about. Tell your friends what Jesus has done for you.

Your friends also need to know what Jesus can do for them. If they've never asked Jesus to forgive them, they need to know He can save them. In the Bible, a man named David asked God to forgive him for a bad thing he did. Then he told God he would teach others God's way and sinners would turn back to God (Ps. 51:13). You can tell your friends how to be saved.

You can do an important job for Jesus: you can tell your friends about Him.

Activity Options

Activity 1: *Witness Bracelet.* This bracelet, based on the wordless book, will help your children be a witness. Give each child a leather strip and one bead of the following colors: black, red, white, and green. Also give them two yellow beads. Children may string the beads on the leather strip in the same order as you talk about the colors: Yellow—God wants everyone to be with Him in heaven; black—everyone has sinned; red—Jesus died for our sins; white—He saves us from our sins; green—we can grow to be like Him; yellow—we can live in heaven with Jesus. Tie a knot on either side of the line of beads so they won't fall off. Tie the thong loosely to the children's wrists. Encourage the children to share their bracelets with others.

Activity 2: *Witness practice.* Let your children practice telling others about Jesus by letting them take turns telling the class what Jesus has done for them. Give your testimony as well.

Action Point

Telling your friends about Jesus is an important job. Can you think of someone you can tell? Will you tell them what Jesus did for you?

Prayer

Dear God, thank You for Jesus and all He has done for us. Help us to be ready to share with our friends what You've done for us. Thank You for letting us help with this important job. Amen.

For Next Time

We tell our friends about Jesus because He makes us feel happy when we know Him. Find out more about that next time.

The Christian Life

Memory Verse
I will be joyful
in God my Savior.
Habakkuk 3:18

 51 I am joyful because
I know Jesus.

Before You Begin

- Read Romans 15:13, Galatians 5:22–26, and Philippians 4:4–7.
- Review the Teaching Points to familiarize yourself with the ideas to emphasize in this session.
- Read the session plan and select the elements that you will include.
- Choose a Bible memorization technique from those listed in Section 1. Be sure to vary your teaching technique from session to session.
- If you choose to include a learning activity, gather the materials you will need.
  - For Activity 1 you will need a glass jar, stones, and pretty marbles or glass beads.

Teaching Points

- I am joyful because I know Jesus.
- Joy comes from knowing Jesus.
- Joy is more than a feeling.
- You can trust Jesus no matter what your feelings are.

Say

Everyone likes to feel happy. We feel happy when things are going well. Happiness is a feeling that comes and goes. But there is a different kind of happiness that we can have deep down inside, and it will never go away. It's called joy. And true joy comes from knowing Jesus.

When we ask Jesus to come into our lives, He takes away all the bad things we've done. But we also get some things when we come to know Jesus. The Bible lists them as "love, joy, peace, patience, kindness, goodness, faithfulness, gentleness and self control" (Gal. 5: 22–23). One of the good things in the list is joy. Joy is more than a feeling. It is a deep happiness we have because we know that Jesus is with us.

We can't always feel happy. Sometimes we feel sad. Sometimes we feel mad. But no matter how we feel, we can know that Jesus is with us. That gives us joy. The Bible says, "May the God of hope fill you with all joy and peace as you trust in him" (Rom. 15:13). You can trust Jesus no matter what your feelings are. Put your trust in Jesus. When you truly know Him, you'll be truly joyful.

Activity Options

Activity 1: *Give and Take.* Show the children a clear glass jar with some stones inside. Talk about how God can remove lying, cheating, bad attitudes, etc. Remove a rock for each sin you talk about. Keep going until the glass is empty. Then talk about the good things listed in Galatians that God can add to our lives. For each one you mention, put a pretty marble or glass bead in the jar. Explain how God takes sin out of our lives and replaces it with good things if we'll come to Him.

Activity 2: *True joy.* Help your children understand the difference between feeling happy and having true joy. Have the children sit down. Suggest to them the different scenarios, and tell the class to jump up when they recognize true joy. Some scenarios you might mention include getting a new toy (happiness); being saved from sin (joy); eating your favorite meal (happiness); and being helped by Jesus to do right (joy).

Action Point

Can you tell the difference between feelings of happiness and true joy? You can have real joy. Ask Jesus into your heart today.

Prayer

Dear God, thank You for giving us a joy that doesn't go away. Help each of us to know Jesus and keep living to please Him so that we might know true joy. Amen.

For Next Time

We can rest in the joy of knowing Jesus is in our lives, but the joy we have now will be even greater someday. Find out how next time.

The Christian Life

Memory Verse
Whoever lives
and believes in me
will never die.
John 11:26

52 I will go to heaven with Jesus.

Before You Begin

- Read Isaiah 35:8–10, Luke 23:39–43, and Revelation 21:1–22:6.
- Review the Teaching Points to familiarize yourself with the ideas to emphasize in this session.
- Read the session plan and select the elements that you will include.
- Choose a Bible memorization technique from those listed in Section 1. Be sure to vary your teaching technique from session to session.
- If you choose to include a learning activity, gather the materials you will need.
  - For Activity 1 you will need a snack.
  - For Activity 2 you will need drawing paper and crayons.

Teaching Points

- We can go to heaven with Jesus.
- Heaven is for those who know Jesus.
- We can choose to go to heaven.
- We need to be ready to go to heaven.

Say

Jesus is in heaven preparing a place for us to be with Him someday. What do you think of when you think of heaven? Heaven is a place God is preparing for those who know him. It is a place where there is no sin. Only those who've asked Jesus to forgive their sins can go there. The Bible says that "nothing impure will ever enter it, nor will anyone who does what is shameful" (Rev. 21:27). Heaven is for those who know Jesus.

Anyone who asks Jesus to forgive them and gives up sinning can go to heaven. When Jesus was dying on the cross, there was a thief hanging on another cross beside Him. He asked Jesus to forgive his sins. Jesus said to the man, "I tell you the truth, today you will be with me in paradise" (Luke 23:43). That man chose to go to heaven by asking Jesus to be his Savior. You can choose to go to heaven too.

Have you ever been excited to go on a trip? Perhaps you got ready very early, but then you had to wait until it was time to go. Heaven is so wonderful that you may wish you could go there now. None of us knows when we'll go to heaven. We need to be ready so we can go when the time comes. We are ready if we've asked Jesus into our hearts to forgive our sins. If you're ready, you will go to heaven with Jesus.

Activity Options

Activity 1: *The ready game.* Tell the children you are leaving the room, but when you come back, you'll take them somewhere, so they must get ready to go. Give them certain tasks to get ready, such as pushing their chairs up to the table, collecting their Bibles and papers, and standing by the door, ready to go. Come back into the room unannounced and see if the children are ready and waiting. Use this activity to demonstrate how we need to be ready at all times to go to heaven. Then, take all the children to another area and serve a snack. (Never leave children unattended. Be sure an adult is in the room with children at all times.)

Activity 2: *Heaven.* Give the children drawing paper and crayons and let them use their imaginations to draw what they think heaven will be like. Talk about some of the descriptions of heaven in Revelation 21–22. Encourage the children to put themselves into the picture. They may also wish to add friends, family members, and Jesus to their picture of heaven.

Action Point

Heaven is a special place God is preparing for those who know Jesus. Are you ready to go to heaven?

Prayer

Dear God, thank You for a place like heaven where there is no sin and we can be with You. Help us to be ready to go there when the time comes by trusting Jesus to be our Savior. Amen.

Development Characteristics of Preschoolers

Preschoolers are on the verge of a world of discovery. They are full of potential, promise, and hope. According to R. S. Lee, author of *Your Growing Children and Religion*, "The first seven years [of life] constitute the period for laying the foundations of religion." Building a solid foundation for a life of spiritual formation is crucial in these young years.

Characteristics

Preschoolers require a loving, safe, and secure relationship. Your actions and attitudes will tell the preschoolers in your care far more about God than your words ever will.

Mental

Children think concretely based on the present, as they have no mental history. They love to explore, examine, and learn using their five senses. Early problem solving skills are being developed and need to be encouraged through leading questions.

Social

Preschoolers are beginning the process of moving away from egocentric play to interactive or associative play. Encourage them to play with friends.

Emotional

Preschoolers tend to be less outwardly emotional. They are beginning to notice others reactions and responses and take on the role of observer. It might be more difficult to get this age to respond and react in a large group setting.

Spiritual

Children are imitators of adults. They feel and understand but without rational thought. They have a simple faith and a strong sense of what is right and wrong. They enjoy and need consistent, solid rules.

Physical

Preschoolers enjoy movement, exploring, and interacting. They are gaining more control over large muscle groups and beginning to add small muscle groups. Cutting, holding pencils, coloring, etc. are getting easier to perform.

Multiple Intelligence

Dr. Howard Gardner from Harvard University developed a theory stating that we all learn through eight different intelligences. Traditional education generally only teaches two of these. The goal of the teacher is to implement as many of these forms of teaching into the classroom setting.

- Verbal/Linguistic—Learn through hearing stories, reading, writing, and memorizing.

- Logical/Mathematical—Learn with numbers, are logical thinkers, need organization, and are problem solvers. They ask a lot of questions.

- Visual/Spatial—Learn through seeing drawings, pictures, colorful bulletin boards, and by painting, drawing, and sculpting. These kids love videos and making art projects.

- Musical/Rhythmic—Music, sound, rhythm, and pitch help these students learn. These preschoolers can remember things through singing them.

- Bodily/Kinesthetic—These are your physical, athletic kids. They enjoy games, movement, and acting.

- Introspective—These kids are very reflective, self-motivated, and enjoy time alone. They will learn through one-on-one interaction, quiet reflection, and independent study. They are often mislabeled as "shy."

- Interpersonal—These kids are the talkative, friendly, outgoing ones. They learn best in group settings and enjoy social times and parties.

- Naturalist—There learn through being outdoors and experiencing nature. They will enjoy field trips, a class pet, and classifying information. When the sun is out, they'll want to be outside.

By being able to recognize in your students where their intelligence lies (most of us use several of these), we can better understand what will inspire them to learn and keep them active learners rather than disruptive bystanders.

Learning Styles

When developing your lesson, you need to be conscious of the following four learning styles and try to incorporate as many as you can into each lesson. People generally tend to teach toward their own learning style. Constant teaching using only one style will encourage discipline problems within the classroom.

Visual Learners

Visual learners need to see what you're talking about. Include bulletin boards, charts, graphs, pictures, and lots of color.

Auditory Learners

These children learn through hearing. They will respond well to verbal directions, use music, and even the "learning noise" in the classroom. They might need to hear their own voice in order to learn. Understand that sound is comforting to them.

Tactile Learners

Tactile learners need to touch and feel what they are learning. Having something they can hold onto or make with their hands while learning will enhance their experience.

Kinesthetic Learners

These children learn through using their whole self. These kids need movement and activity. Include large muscle activities and drama to encourage them to learn.

The best way to determine the learning style of a child is to observe them in the classroom. See what activities and learning experiences they favor. If a student is having a behavior problem, try to include a tactile or kinesthetic experience and see if they respond positively.

Preschool Assessment Tool

1. What is God like?

God is real.
God is good.
God can do anything.
God knows everything.
God can hear us talk to Him.

2. What did God make?

God made the world.
(They may list lots of individual items.)
God made me.

3. What is God's special book?

The Bible.

4. What can we learn about in the Bible?

The Bible tells us about God and Jesus.
The stories in the Bible are true.
The Bible helps me know what to do.
The Bible teaches me how to live.

5. What does God do for you?

God made me special.
God loves me.
God made my family.

6. Who is Jesus?

Jesus is God's son.

7. How did Jesus come to Earth?

Jesus was born as a baby.

8. What did Jesus do here on Earth?

Jesus grew up, just like me.
Jesus obeyed God.
Jesus taught people about God.

9. How does Jesus feel about you?

Jesus loves me!

10. What did Jesus do for you?

Jesus died on the cross.

11. Why did Jesus die on the cross?

Jesus died on the cross to pay for sin.

12. Is Jesus still dead?

No—Jesus is alive!
Jesus is in heaven.

13. What is sin?

Sin is doing wrong.

14. Who has sinned?

Everyone has sinned.

15. What should we do about sin?

Ask God to forgive us.

16. What does Jesus want to be?

Jesus (wants to be) is my forever friend.

17. What do we do at church?

We worship God. (We show God how much we love Him.)
We learn about Jesus.
We sing and pray.
We read the Bible.
We help other people.
We bring offerings.

18. What can I do for God?

I can invite a friend to church.
I can help others.
I can grow like Jesus. (I can share love like Jesus. I can love like Jesus. I can care like Jesus.)
I can love my family.
I can tell my friends about Jesus.

Preschool Scripture Memory Ideas

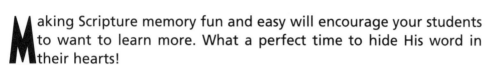

Making Scripture memory fun and easy will encourage your students to want to learn more. What a perfect time to hide His word in their hearts!

Try to vary your method—try new ones, and come up with your own. Let the kids invent a new method too! The more engaged the students are, the better chance of the Scripture verse becoming a memory verse. Remember preschoolers will need symbols or pictures to represent the words, as they are non-readers. Positive words, praise, and encouragement for true effort, as well as success, are important at this age level.

Picture This

Create a picture or symbol for the major words in the memory verse. This creates a visual image for the students and will help them "read" the verse with you. Allow the students time to color their own copies of the picture verse or draw it for themselves.

Envelope Mix-Up

Put each picture and word of a memory verse on a separate piece of paper. Mix the pieces of paper and put them into an envelope. Make up enough envelopes to give one to each person or pair of people in your group. The first person or pair to put the words of the memory verse in the correct order is the winner.

Push Pin Review

Have each picture word of a memory verse written on a three-by-five-inch card or a piece of paper. Show the students the verse with the picture cards in order. Take the cards down and allow the students to reassemble the cards in order themselves. Try to allow each student to have a turn.

Make a Match

Create two sets of picture cards for each word (phrase) for the memory verse. Say the verse together as you show them the two sets of cards. Turn the cards over and have students take turns trying to find each picture word's match. When all matches have been found, say the verse together again.

Whiteboard Erase

Draw the memory verse in pictures on the whiteboard. Have someone (or the entire group) "read" the verse. Then erase pictures one at a time. Have the class recite the verse again. Continue to do this until all of the pictures are gone.

Around the Table Memory

Have the group sit in a circle. Give each student a picture representing a word or phrase from the memory verse. Start at the beginning of the verse and have each student say his or her picture word in turn to complete the verse. Gradually increase speed so that the group must recite the verse faster and faster. At some point, remove the pictures so that the group must recite the verse from memory.

Create a Cheer

Turn the Scripture verse into a cheer. Create a cheer from the words of the memory verse by adding motions, phrasing, repetition, and intonation that will turn "Go ye into all the world..." into a motivational cheer. Encourage creativity, movement, and be prepared for laughter.

Sing a Song

Many of us learn better when we sing. Turn the memory verse into a song by using a familiar tune. Make it a chant, a rap, or a simple melody. Many verses have already been turned into songs or worship choruses. These are great to use to teach the memory verse. The students will have fun singing and learning.

Moving Memory

Kids need to move, and they love to use their hands. Add motions or use sign language to get kids moving, and relate each key word or phrase to a movement. They'll remember the movement and then remember the word. When you do this, don't try to have a move or sign for every word, which can get too busy and confusing. Keep the motions simple and basic. Let the kids be creative and help you design the moves.

Prop Up Memory

Use objects or props to represent key words or phrases that will help the kids remember. Connecting an every day object to a memory verse word will help them make a mental picture of the verse—a picture they can carry with them. You can select the props ahead of time, and let the kids help you "prop up" the memory verse. Or you can let the kids choose the objects and then search the church for them. They'll enjoy the search as well as putting it all together. The entire process will imprint the words, phrases, and meaning in their minds.

Sign and Say

Help children remember the memory verse by learning to say it with sign language. Seek assistance from someone in your church or community or go to http://commtechlab.msu.edu/sites/aslweb/browser.htm.

How to Lead a Child to Christ

As you present the lessons in this book, the opportunity will arise for you to ask the students if they have a personal relationship with Jesus Christ. If they do not, please carefully consider these suggestions.

1. Be sensitive to the leading of the Holy Spirit in the child's life. Conversion is the work of the Holy Spirit. God will draw children to himself. Never force, coerce, or push children to make a decision. Salvation must be freely accepted. Be prepared for teachable moments.

2. Pray for the child. Pray for open doors to share the gospel (Col. 4:2–4). Pray that God will prepare their hearts and make you sensitive to the opportunities.

3. Understand when the child is ready. When a child understands that God is a being who loves him or her, when a child can know the difference between right and wrong, when he or she experiences sorrow for doing wrong, and when the child gains a basic understanding of Jesus as God's Son who died for his or her sin, then that child is ready to respond!

4. Know how to explain the plan of salvation. Here is a method for presenting the gospel to children:

Jesus wants children to come to Him (Mark 10:14–15).
God loves you and sent Jesus to die for you (John 3:16).
You have sinned against God (Rom. 3:23).
The penalty for sin is death (Rom. 6:23).
You can ask Jesus to take away your sins (Rom. 5:8).
You can receive the forgiveness of sins (1 John 1:9).
You can become a member of God's family (John 1:12).

5. Help the child pray to express faith in Christ. Here is a simple prayer you might use: "Dear Jesus, I know I have sinned, and I am sorry. I turn away from my sins and ask You to forgive me. I believe You are God's Son and that You died for my sins. I confess my sins to You, and now

I want to receive You into my life as my friend and Savior. Thank You, Jesus. Amen."

6. Rejoice, review, and reaffirm. Celebrate with the child, and give them the opportunity to share with the whole group. Make sure the child's parents know about his or her decision. Encourage parents to read to them from the Bible daily and to model prayer and regular church attendance.

How to Teach Children to Pray

Children are very open, and their hearts are pure. Model childlike-faith prayers, be patient with childish requests and needs, encourage open, honest prayers, and allow children to grow through frequent and consistent prayer time.

Below are a few simple techniques to help vary your class prayer time and encourage students to directly participate.

Sentence Prayers

Have children take turns saying one-sentence prayers. A specific idea or topic can be suggested or left open-ended.

Circle Prayers

Have children hold hands and stand in a circle. Go around the circle, praying for the person on their right. (If they aren't comfortable praying out loud, they can squeeze the next person's hand to pass.)

One-Word Prayers

Begin with a sentence and allow children to fill in at random and out loud with one word. For example, you might say, "Jesus we thank You for . . ." or "Heavenly Father, help us this week to . . . ."

Prayer Requests

Allow a time of sharing needs, concerns, and requests. After each request, ask or assign a specific student to pray.

Open Prayer Time

Tell the students you are going to allow them to speak out if they would like to pray. Have everyone close their eyes. Wait for their responses, and then close in a final prayer.

Hands-On Prayers

If a student is having a specific struggle, serious illness, or situation, have the class gather around them, laying hands on them and praying out loud.

Partner Prayers or Small Group Prayers

If you have a large group of students, have them pair up or form small groups. Share requests and take turns praying for one another.

Silent Prayers

Introduce a specific need or prayer idea. Then give students a few moments of individual, silent prayer time before you or a selected student closes with an audible prayer.

Written Prayers

Create a prayer wall or board. Provide students with cards or notes on which to write their prayers, requests, or praises.

Modeling Prayer

Provide examples of prayers to your students by praying for them. Be conscious to make your prayers conversational—using language and verbiage the students would be comfortable using. Make sure you include praise, thanks, reflection, and requests.

Listening Prayers

Help students understand that prayer is not just talking to God but includes waiting and being still for Him to talk to us. Provide opportunities where students are quiet and still before God, allowing Him to speak to them.

Music Resources

A child's spiritual development must include opportunities to worship. Worship can include a variety of elements as we commune with God and He with us. Children's corporate worship should be done reverently, actively, and joyfully.

Typical elements of worship include prayer, bringing offerings, sharing praises, reading the Word, sharing a special song, a creative movement, drama, art, and music.

Below is a list of resources that can assist you in your worship through music:

- "Grow, Grow, Grow" by Karyn Henley. CD includes 12 songs that celebrates the excitement of gaining new skills and knowledge.

- "Five Little Ladybugs" by Karyn Henley. 11 songs where children celebrate God's creation.

- "Shout to the Lord" Volumes 1, 2, 3, 4 by Integrity Music. Contemporary worship songs sung with and for kids.

- "i WORSHIP kids" by Integrity Music. High energy worship music typical of Integrity's "i Worship" but recorded especially for kids.

- "Great Big Praise" (Book One) Publisher, Lillenas Music.

- "Scripture Rock" by Provident Music. CD contains 50 Scripture verses set to a fun rock style.

- "Songs 4 Worship Kids" by Integrity. Multiple CD set includes many of today's popular worship songs and some new titles.

- "MOVE It Like This" by ZonderKidz CD and instructional DVD contain 10 songs from fast paced to slow and reverent for kids.

- "The Kids' Hymns Project" by Lillenas. Fifteen hymns arranged for children in an exciting, contemporary style.

Additional Resources

Discipleship

NowThat I'm a Christian Bible Studies for Children by Donna Fillmore

Awesome Adventure by Through the Bible Publishers

Beyond Belief by Josh McDowell and Ron Luce

Child Development

Child Sensitive Teaching by Karyn Henley

Transforming Children into Spiritual Champions by George Barna

The Faith of a Child by Art Murphy

Opening Your Child's Nine Learning Windows by Cheri Fuller

The Disconnected Generation by Josh McDowell

Teaching on Target by Group Publishing

Is It a Lost Cause? Having the Heart of God for the Church's Children by Marva J. Dawn

Bringing Up Boys by Dr. James Dobson

Creative Teaching Methods by Marlene D. LeFever

The Five Love Languages of Children by Gary Chapman and Ross Campbell, M.D.

Early Childhood Smart Pages by Sheryl Haystead

Instructional Aids

Sword Fighting by Karyn Henley

How to Study Your Bible for Kids by Kay Arthur and Janna Arndt

The Big Book of Bible Skills by Gospel Light

Children's Ministry Resource Bible published by Child Evangelism Fellowship

Making Scripture Memory Fun by Group Publishing

801 Questions Kids Ask about God with Answers from the Bible by Focus on the Family

1001 Ways to Introduce Your Child to the Bible by Kathie Reimer

What the Bible Is All about for Young Explorers published by Gospel Light

Kidcordance Big Ideas from the Bible and Where to Find Them published by Zonderkidz

Bibles

The NIV Adventure Bible published by Zonderkidz

KidsBible.com New Century Version published by Nelson Bibles for Kids

The Beginners Bible published by Gold'n'Honey Books

The Growing Reader Phonics Bible published by Tyndale Kids

Pray & Play Bible published by Group

Pray & Play Bible 2 published by Group

Preschool Resources

The Preschooler Worker's Encyclopedia of Bible Teaching Ideas (NT) published by Group

First Favorite Bible Lessons for Preschoolers published by Group

Tippy Towers and Boo Blankets published by Group

Playful Songs & Bible Stories published by Group

Simple Stories Jesus Told by Mary Rich Hopkins

Service Projects Preschoolers Can Do published by Group

Jesus Loves Me published by Group

Age Right Play by Susan L. Lingo

Five Little Ladybugs by Karyn Henley

My God and Me (Little Kids Time) published by Gospel Light

Jesus Loves Me published by Group

Wiggly Giggly Bible Learning Center published by Group

Reproducible
Activities Items

God hears me talk to Him

I remembered to talk to God today

Sunday	Monday	Tuesday	Wednesday	Thursday	Friday	Saturday

What does God see?

The Bible tells me about God and Jesus

133

your Soul

your Heart

your Strength

your Mind

Love the Lord
your God with all...

God's Son

135

Jesus always obeyed God

I can obey God at all times

12 1 2 3 4 5 6 7 8 9 10 11

Who Teaches?

Giving Certificate

Jesus gave Himself to others because He loved them.
I love...

Because I love you, I would like to do this for you:

He is not here;
He is risen, just
as He said.
Matthew 28:6

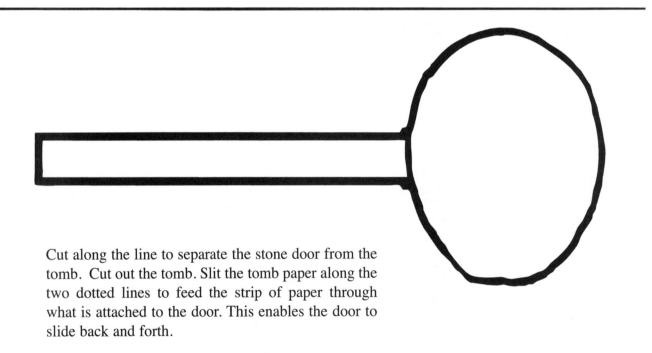

Cut along the line to separate the stone door from the tomb. Cut out the tomb. Slit the tomb paper along the two dotted lines to feed the strip of paper through what is attached to the door. This enables the door to slide back and forth.

God wants to forgive

God wants to forgive

141

Confess

Repent

STOP

Receive

Believe

TEACHING CALENDAR

DATE	CONCEPT	SESSION ELEMENTS	ACTIVITY OPTIONS	TEACHING TOOLS

*See Step 5 in "How to Use This Book" – Create a Teaching Calendar